C-1484

CAREER EXAMINATION SERIES

THIS IS YOUR **PASSBOOK**® FOR ...

SUPERVISOR OF MECHANICS (MECHANICAL EQUIPMENT)

NATIONAL LEARNING CORPORATION®
passbooks.com

COPYRIGHT NOTICE

Copyright © 2018 by

NLC®

National Learning Corporation

212 Michael Drive, Syosset, NY 11791
(516) 921-8888 • www.passbooks.com
E-mail: info@passbooks.com

PUBLISHED IN THE UNITED STATES OF AMERICA

PASSBOOK® SERIES

THE *PASSBOOK® SERIES* has been created to prepare applicants and candidates for the ultimate academic battlefield – the examination room.

At some time in our lives, each and every one of us may be required to take an examination – for validation, matriculation, admission, qualification, registration, certification, or licensure.

Based on the assumption that every applicant or candidate has met the basic formal educational standards, has taken the required number of courses, and read the necessary texts, the *PASSBOOK® SERIES* furnishes the one special preparation which may assure passing with confidence, instead of failing with insecurity. Examination questions – together with answers – are furnished as the basic vehicle for study so that the mysteries of the examination and its compounding difficulties may be eliminated or diminished by a sure method.

This book is meant to help you pass your examination provided that you qualify and are serious in your objective.

The entire field is reviewed through the huge store of content information which is succinctly presented through a provocative and challenging approach – the question-and-answer method.

A climate of success is established by furnishing the correct answers at the end of each test.

You soon learn to recognize types of questions, forms of questions, and patterns of questioning. You may even begin to anticipate expected outcomes.

You perceive that many questions are repeated or adapted so that you can gain acute insights, which may enable you to score many sure points.

You learn how to confront new questions, or types of questions, and to attack them confidently and work out the correct answers.

You note objectives and emphases, and recognize pitfalls and dangers, so that you may make positive educational adjustments.

Moreover, you are kept fully informed in relation to new concepts, methods, practices, and directions in the field.

You discover that you arre actually taking the examination all the time: you are preparing for the examination by "taking" an examination, not by reading extraneous and/or supererogatory textbooks.

In short, this PASSBOOK®, used directedly, should be an important factor in helping you to pass your test.

SUPERVISOR OF MECHANICS (MECHANICAL EQUIPMENT)

JOB DESCRIPTION

Under general supervision or direction, supervises, directs and is responsible for the work of assigned personnel in connection with the repair, overhaul and maintenance of various types of mechanical equipment, motor vehicles and automotive equipment. Supervises assigned personnel. Performs related work.

EXAMPLES OF TYPICAL TASKS

Prepares work schedules and makes assignments. Makes decisions relative to methods of doing work. May interpret mechanical drawings. Makes inspections and checks work progress. Makes recommendations and suggestions regarding the purchasing of production machinery. Insures that an adequate supply of proper parts is maintained in all stockrooms. Initiates purchase of parts and equipment. Contacts vendors to ensure that parts, materials, and equipment are made to specifications and will be delivered on time. Insures that equipment needs are met in assigned area. Is responsible for the maintenance, repair and safeguarding of assigned equipment. Develops, recommends and implements productivity and cost saving measures. Enforces safety precautions. Keeps records and makes reports. Operates motor vehicles in the performance of assigned duties.

TEST

The multiple-choice test may include questions on: planning and organizing; problem identification; problem solving; delegation; monitoring of work procedures; directing others; written communication; record keeping; analyzing and processing numerical and statistical data; technical knowledge relating to the maintenance, repair and safeguarding of vehicles, equipment and related parts and materials; interpretation of personnel policies and procedures; standards of proper employee ethical conduct; and other related areas.

HOW TO TAKE A TEST

I. YOU MUST PASS AN EXAMINATION

A. WHAT EVERY CANDIDATE SHOULD KNOW

Examination applicants often ask us for help in preparing for the written test. What can I study in advance? What kinds of questions will be asked? How will the test be given? How will the papers be graded?

As an applicant for a civil service examination, you may be wondering about some of these things. Our purpose here is to suggest effective methods of advance study and to describe civil service examinations.

Your chances for success on this examination can be increased if you know how to prepare. Those "pre-examination jitters" can be reduced if you know what to expect. You can even experience an adventure in good citizenship if you know why civil service exams are given.

B. WHY ARE CIVIL SERVICE EXAMINATIONS GIVEN?

Civil service examinations are important to you in two ways. As a citizen, you want public jobs filled by employees who know how to do their work. As a job seeker, you want a fair chance to compete for that job on an equal footing with other candidates. The best-known means of accomplishing this two-fold goal is the competitive examination.

Exams are widely publicized throughout the nation. They may be administered for jobs in federal, state, city, municipal, town or village governments or agencies.

Any citizen may apply, with some limitations, such as the age or residence of applicants. Your experience and education may be reviewed to see whether you meet the requirements for the particular examination. When these requirements exist, they are reasonable and applied consistently to all applicants. Thus, a competitive examination may cause you some uneasiness now, but it is your privilege and safeguard.

C. HOW ARE CIVIL SERVICE EXAMS DEVELOPED?

Examinations are carefully written by trained technicians who are specialists in the field known as "psychological measurement," in consultation with recognized authorities in the field of work that the test will cover. These experts recommend the subject matter areas or skills to be tested; only those knowledges or skills important to your success on the job are included. The most reliable books and source materials available are used as references. Together, the experts and technicians judge the difficulty level of the questions.

Test technicians know how to phrase questions so that the problem is clearly stated. Their ethics do not permit "trick" or "catch" questions. Questions may have been tried out on sample groups, or subjected to statistical analysis, to determine their usefulness.

Written tests are often used in combination with performance tests, ratings of training and experience, and oral interviews. All of these measures combine to form the best-known means of finding the right person for the right job.

II. HOW TO PASS THE WRITTEN TEST

A. *NATURE OF THE EXAMINATION*

To prepare intelligently for civil service examinations, you should know how they differ from school examinations you have taken. In school you were assigned certain definite pages to read or subjects to cover. The examination questions were quite detailed and usually emphasized memory. Civil service exams, on the other hand, try to discover your present ability to perform the duties of a position, plus your potentiality to learn these duties. In other words, a civil service exam attempts to predict how successful you will be. Questions cover such a broad area that they cannot be as minute and detailed as school exam questions.

In the public service similar kinds of work, or positions, are grouped together in one "class." This process is known as *position-classification*. All the positions in a class are paid according to the salary range for that class. One class title covers all of these positions, and they are all tested by the same examination.

B. *FOUR BASIC STEPS*

1) Study the announcement

How, then, can you know what subjects to study? Our best answer is: "Learn as much as possible about the class of positions for which you've applied." The exam will test the knowledge, skills and abilities needed to do the work.

Your most valuable source of information about the position you want is the official exam announcement. This announcement lists the training and experience qualifications. Check these standards and apply only if you come reasonably close to meeting them.

The brief description of the position in the examination announcement offers some clues to the subjects which will be tested. Think about the job itself. Review the duties in your mind. Can you perform them, or are there some in which you are rusty? Fill in the blank spots in your preparation.

Many jurisdictions preview the written test in the exam announcement by including a section called "Knowledge and Abilities Required," "Scope of the Examination," or some similar heading. Here you will find out specifically what fields will be tested.

2) Review your own background

Once you learn in general what the position is all about, and what you need to know to do the work, ask yourself which subjects you already know fairly well and which need improvement. You may wonder whether to concentrate on improving your strong areas or on building some background in your fields of weakness. When the announcement has specified "some knowledge" or "considerable knowledge," or has used adjectives like "beginning principles of…" or "advanced … methods," you can get a clue as to the number and difficulty of questions to be asked in any given field. More questions, and hence broader coverage, would be included for those subjects which are more important in the work. Now weigh your strengths and weaknesses against the job requirements and prepare accordingly.

3) Determine the level of the position

Another way to tell how intensively you should prepare is to understand the level of the job for which you are applying. Is it the entering level? In other words, is this the position in which beginners in a field of work are hired? Or is it an intermediate or advanced level? Sometimes this is indicated by such words as "Junior" or "Senior" in the class title. Other jurisdictions use Roman numerals to designate the level – Clerk I, Clerk II, for example. The word "Supervisor" sometimes appears in the title. If the level is not indicated by the title, check the description of duties. Will you be working under very close supervision, or will you have responsibility for independent decisions in this work?

4) Choose appropriate study materials

Now that you know the subjects to be examined and the relative amount of each subject to be covered, you can choose suitable study materials. For beginning level jobs, or even advanced ones, if you have a pronounced weakness in some aspect of your training, read a modern, standard textbook in that field. Be sure it is up to date and has general coverage. Such books are normally available at your library, and the librarian will be glad to help you locate one. For entry-level positions, questions of appropriate difficulty are chosen – neither highly advanced questions, nor those too simple. Such questions require careful thought but not advanced training.

If the position for which you are applying is technical or advanced, you will read more advanced, specialized material. If you are already familiar with the basic principles of your field, elementary textbooks would waste your time. Concentrate on advanced textbooks and technical periodicals. Think through the concepts and review difficult problems in your field.

These are all general sources. You can get more ideas on your own initiative, following these leads. For example, training manuals and publications of the government agency which employs workers in your field can be useful, particularly for technical and professional positions. A letter or visit to the government department involved may result in more specific study suggestions, and certainly will provide you with a more definite idea of the exact nature of the position you are seeking.

III. KINDS OF TESTS

Tests are used for purposes other than measuring knowledge and ability to perform specified duties. For some positions, it is equally important to test ability to make adjustments to new situations or to profit from training. In others, basic mental abilities not dependent on information are essential. Questions which test these things may not appear as pertinent to the duties of the position as those which test for knowledge and information. Yet they are often highly important parts of a fair examination. For very general questions, it is almost impossible to help you direct your study efforts. What we can do is to point out some of the more common of these general abilities needed in public service positions and describe some typical questions.

1) General information

Broad, general information has been found useful for predicting job success in some kinds of work. This is tested in a variety of ways, from vocabulary lists to questions about current events. Basic background in some field of work, such as sociology or economics, may be sampled in a group of questions. Often these are principles which have become familiar to most persons through exposure rather than through formal training. It is difficult to advise you how to study for these questions; being alert to the world around you is our best suggestion.

2) Verbal ability

An example of an ability needed in many positions is verbal or language ability. Verbal ability is, in brief, the ability to use and understand words. Vocabulary and grammar tests are typical measures of this ability. Reading comprehension or paragraph interpretation questions are common in many kinds of civil service tests. You are given a paragraph of written material and asked to find its central meaning.

3) Numerical ability

Number skills can be tested by the familiar arithmetic problem, by checking paired lists of numbers to see which are alike and which are different, or by interpreting charts and graphs. In the latter test, a graph may be printed in the test booklet which you are asked to use as the basis for answering questions.

4) Observation

A popular test for law-enforcement positions is the observation test. A picture is shown to you for several minutes, then taken away. Questions about the picture test your ability to observe both details and larger elements.

5) Following directions

In many positions in the public service, the employee must be able to carry out written instructions dependably and accurately. You may be given a chart with several columns, each column listing a variety of information. The questions require you to carry out directions involving the information given in the chart.

6) Skills and aptitudes

Performance tests effectively measure some manual skills and aptitudes. When the skill is one in which you are trained, such as typing or shorthand, you can practice. These tests are often very much like those given in business school or high school courses. For many of the other skills and aptitudes, however, no short-time preparation can be made. Skills and abilities natural to you or that you have developed throughout your lifetime are being tested.

Many of the general questions just described provide all the data needed to answer the questions and ask you to use your reasoning ability to find the answers. Your best preparation for these tests, as well as for tests of facts and ideas, is to be at your physical and mental best. You, no doubt, have your own methods of getting into an exam-taking mood and keeping "in shape." The next section lists some ideas on this subject.

IV. KINDS OF QUESTIONS

Only rarely is the "essay" question, which you answer in narrative form, used in civil service tests. Civil service tests are usually of the short-answer type. Full instructions for answering these questions will be given to you at the examination. But in case this is your first experience with short-answer questions and separate answer sheets, here is what you need to know:

1) Multiple-choice Questions

Most popular of the short-answer questions is the "multiple choice" or "best answer" question. It can be used, for example, to test for factual knowledge, ability to solve problems or judgment in meeting situations found at work.

A multiple-choice question is normally one of three types—

- It can begin with an incomplete statement followed by several possible endings. You are to find the one ending which *best* completes the statement, although some of the others may not be entirely wrong.
- It can also be a complete statement in the form of a question which is answered by choosing one of the statements listed.
- It can be in the form of a problem – again you select the best answer.

Here is an example of a multiple-choice question with a discussion which should give you some clues as to the method for choosing the right answer:

When an employee has a complaint about his assignment, the action which will *best* help him overcome his difficulty is to
    A. discuss his difficulty with his coworkers
    B. take the problem to the head of the organization
    C. take the problem to the person who gave him the assignment
    D. say nothing to anyone about his complaint

In answering this question, you should study each of the choices to find which is best. Consider choice "A" – Certainly an employee may discuss his complaint with fellow employees, but no change or improvement can result, and the complaint remains unresolved. Choice "B" is a poor choice since the head of the organization probably does not know what assignment you have been given, and taking your problem to him is known as "going over the head" of the supervisor. The supervisor, or person who made the assignment, is the person who can clarify it or correct any injustice. Choice "C" is, therefore, correct. To say nothing, as in choice "D," is unwise. Supervisors have and interest in knowing the problems employees are facing, and the employee is seeking a solution to his problem.

2) True/False Questions

The "true/false" or "right/wrong" form of question is sometimes used. Here a complete statement is given. Your job is to decide whether the statement is right or wrong.

SAMPLE: A roaming cell-phone call to a nearby city costs less than a non-roaming call to a distant city.

This statement is wrong, or false, since roaming calls are more expensive.

This is not a complete list of all possible question forms, although most of the others are variations of these common types. You will always get complete directions for answering questions. Be sure you understand *how* to mark your answers – ask questions until you do.

V. RECORDING YOUR ANSWERS

Computer terminals are used more and more today for many different kinds of exams.

For an examination with very few applicants, you may be told to record your answers in the test booklet itself. Separate answer sheets are much more common. If this separate answer sheet is to be scored by machine – and this is often the case – it is highly important that you mark your answers correctly in order to get credit.

An electronic scoring machine is often used in civil service offices because of the speed with which papers can be scored. Machine-scored answer sheets must be marked with a pencil, which will be given to you. This pencil has a high graphite content which responds to the electronic scoring machine. As a matter of fact, stray dots may register as answers, so do not let your pencil rest on the answer sheet while you are pondering the correct answer. Also, if your pencil lead breaks or is otherwise defective, ask for another.

Since the answer sheet will be dropped in a slot in the scoring machine, be careful not to bend the corners or get the paper crumpled.

The answer sheet normally has five vertical columns of numbers, with 30 numbers to a column. These numbers correspond to the question numbers in your test booklet. After each number, going across the page are four or five pairs of dotted lines. These short dotted lines have small letters or numbers above them. The first two pairs may also have a "T" or "F" above the letters. This indicates that the first two pairs only are to be used if the questions are of the true-false type. If the questions are multiple choice, disregard the "T" and "F" and pay attention only to the small letters or numbers.

Answer your questions in the manner of the sample that follows:

32. The largest city in the United States is
   A. Washington, D.C.
   B. New York City
   C. Chicago
   D. Detroit
   E. San Francisco

1) Choose the answer you think is best. (New York City is the largest, so "B" is correct.)
2) Find the row of dotted lines numbered the same as the question you are answering. (Find row number 32)
3) Find the pair of dotted lines corresponding to the answer. (Find the pair of lines under the mark "B.")
4) Make a solid black mark between the dotted lines.

VI. BEFORE THE TEST

Common sense will help you find procedures to follow to get ready for an examination. Too many of us, however, overlook these sensible measures. Indeed, nervousness and fatigue have been found to be the most serious reasons why applicants fail to do their best on civil service tests. Here is a list of reminders:

- Begin your preparation early – Don't wait until the last minute to go scurrying around for books and materials or to find out what the position is all about.
- Prepare continuously – An hour a night for a week is better than an all-night cram session. This has been definitely established. What is more, a night a week for a month will return better dividends than crowding your study into a shorter period of time.
- Locate the place of the exam – You have been sent a notice telling you when and where to report for the examination. If the location is in a different town or otherwise unfamiliar to you, it would be well to inquire the best route and learn something about the building.
- Relax the night before the test – Allow your mind to rest. Do not study at all that night. Plan some mild recreation or diversion; then go to bed early and get a good night's sleep.
- Get up early enough to make a leisurely trip to the place for the test – This way unforeseen events, traffic snarls, unfamiliar buildings, etc. will not upset you.
- Dress comfortably – A written test is not a fashion show. You will be known by number and not by name, so wear something comfortable.
- Leave excess paraphernalia at home – Shopping bags and odd bundles will get in your way. You need bring only the items mentioned in the official notice you received; usually everything you need is provided. Do not bring reference books to the exam. They will only confuse those last minutes and be taken away from you when in the test room.
- Arrive somewhat ahead of time – If because of transportation schedules you must get there very early, bring a newspaper or magazine to take your mind off yourself while waiting.
- Locate the examination room – When you have found the proper room, you will be directed to the seat or part of the room where you will sit. Sometimes you are given a sheet of instructions to read while you are waiting. Do not fill out any forms until you are told to do so; just read them and be prepared.
- Relax and prepare to listen to the instructions
- If you have any physical problem that may keep you from doing your best, be sure to tell the test administrator. If you are sick or in poor health, you really cannot do your best on the exam. You can come back and take the test some other time.

VII. AT THE TEST

The day of the test is here and you have the test booklet in your hand. The temptation to get going is very strong. Caution! There is more to success than knowing the right answers. You must know how to identify your papers and understand variations in the type of short-answer question used in this particular examination. Follow these suggestions for maximum results from your efforts:

1) Cooperate with the monitor

The test administrator has a duty to create a situation in which you can be as much at ease as possible. He will give instructions, tell you when to begin, check to see that you are marking your answer sheet correctly, and so on. He is not there to guard you, although he will see that your competitors do not take unfair advantage. He wants to help you do your best.

2) Listen to all instructions

Don't jump the gun! Wait until you understand all directions. In most civil service tests you get more time than you need to answer the questions. So don't be in a hurry. Read each word of instructions until you clearly understand the meaning. Study the examples, listen to all announcements and follow directions. Ask questions if you do not understand what to do.

3) Identify your papers

Civil service exams are usually identified by number only. You will be assigned a number; you must not put your name on your test papers. Be sure to copy your number correctly. Since more than one exam may be given, copy your exact examination title.

4) Plan your time

Unless you are told that a test is a "speed" or "rate of work" test, speed itself is usually not important. Time enough to answer all the questions will be provided, but this does not mean that you have all day. An overall time limit has been set. Divide the total time (in minutes) by the number of questions to determine the approximate time you have for each question.

5) Do not linger over difficult questions

If you come across a difficult question, mark it with a paper clip (useful to have along) and come back to it when you have been through the booklet. One caution if you do this – be sure to skip a number on your answer sheet as well. Check often to be sure that you have not lost your place and that you are marking in the row numbered the same as the question you are answering.

6) Read the questions

Be sure you know what the question asks! Many capable people are unsuccessful because they failed to *read* the questions correctly.

7) Answer all questions

Unless you have been instructed that a penalty will be deducted for incorrect answers, it is better to guess than to omit a question.

8) Speed tests

It is often better NOT to guess on speed tests. It has been found that on timed tests people are tempted to spend the last few seconds before time is called in marking answers at random – without even reading them – in the hope of picking up a few extra points. To discourage this practice, the instructions may warn you that your score will be "corrected" for guessing. That is, a penalty will be applied. The incorrect answers will be deducted from the correct ones, or some other penalty formula will be used.

9) Review your answers

If you finish before time is called, go back to the questions you guessed or omitted to give them further thought. Review other answers if you have time.

10) Return your test materials

If you are ready to leave before others have finished or time is called, take ALL your materials to the monitor and leave quietly. Never take any test material with you. The monitor can discover whose papers are not complete, and taking a test booklet may be grounds for disqualification.

VIII. EXAMINATION TECHNIQUES

1) Read the general instructions carefully. These are usually printed on the first page of the exam booklet. As a rule, these instructions refer to the timing of the examination; the fact that you should not start work until the signal and must stop work at a signal, etc. If there are any *special* instructions, such as a choice of questions to be answered, make sure that you note this instruction carefully.

2) When you are ready to start work on the examination, that is as soon as the signal has been given, read the instructions to each question booklet, underline any key words or phrases, such as *least, best, outline, describe* and the like. In this way you will tend to answer as requested rather than discover on reviewing your paper that you *listed without describing*, that you selected the *worst* choice rather than the *best* choice, etc.

3) If the examination is of the objective or multiple-choice type – that is, each question will also give a series of possible answers: A, B, C or D, and you are called upon to select the best answer and write the letter next to that answer on your answer paper – it is advisable to start answering each question in turn. There may be anywhere from 50 to 100 such questions in the three or four hours allotted and you can see how much time would be taken if you read through all the questions before beginning to answer any. Furthermore, if you come across a question or group of questions which you know would be difficult to answer, it would undoubtedly affect your handling of all the other questions.

4) If the examination is of the essay type and contains but a few questions, it is a moot point as to whether you should read all the questions before starting to answer any one. Of course, if you are given a choice – say five out of seven and the like – then it is essential to read all the questions so you can eliminate the two that are most difficult. If, however, you are asked to answer all the questions, there may be danger in trying to answer the easiest one first because you may find that you will spend too much time on it. The best technique is to answer the first question, then proceed to the second, etc.

5) Time your answers. Before the exam begins, write down the time it started, then add the time allowed for the examination and write down the time it must be completed, then divide the time available somewhat as follows:

- If 3-1/2 hours are allowed, that would be 210 minutes. If you have 80 objective-type questions, that would be an average of 2-1/2 minutes per question. Allow yourself no more than 2 minutes per question, or a total of 160 minutes, which will permit about 50 minutes to review.
- If for the time allotment of 210 minutes there are 7 essay questions to answer, that would average about 30 minutes a question. Give yourself only 25 minutes per question so that you have about 35 minutes to review.

6) The most important instruction is to *read each question* and make sure you know what is wanted. The second most important instruction is to *time yourself properly* so that you answer every question. The third most important instruction is to *answer every question*. Guess if you have to but include something for each question. Remember that you will receive no credit for a blank and will probably receive some credit if you write something in answer to an essay question. If you guess a letter – say "B" for a multiple-choice question – you may have guessed right. If you leave a blank as an answer to a multiple-choice question, the examiners may respect your feelings but it will not add a point to your score. Some exams may penalize you for wrong answers, so in such cases *only*, you may not want to guess unless you have some basis for your answer.

7) Suggestions
  a. Objective-type questions
    1. Examine the question booklet for proper sequence of pages and questions
    2. Read all instructions carefully
    3. Skip any question which seems too difficult; return to it after all other questions have been answered
    4. Apportion your time properly; do not spend too much time on any single question or group of questions
    5. Note and underline key words – *all, most, fewest, least, best, worst, same, opposite,* etc.
    6. Pay particular attention to negatives
    7. Note unusual option, e.g., unduly long, short, complex, different or similar in content to the body of the question
    8. Observe the use of "hedging" words – *probably, may, most likely,* etc.
    9. Make sure that your answer is put next to the same number as the question
    10. Do not second-guess unless you have good reason to believe the second answer is definitely more correct
    11. Cross out original answer if you decide another answer is more accurate; do not erase until you are ready to hand your paper in
    12. Answer all questions; guess unless instructed otherwise
    13. Leave time for review

  b. Essay questions
    1. Read each question carefully
    2. Determine exactly what is wanted. Underline key words or phrases.
    3. Decide on outline or paragraph answer

4. Include many different points and elements unless asked to develop any one or two points or elements
5. Show impartiality by giving pros and cons unless directed to select one side only
6. Make and write down any assumptions you find necessary to answer the questions
7. Watch your English, grammar, punctuation and choice of words
8. Time your answers; don't crowd material

8) Answering the essay question

Most essay questions can be answered by framing the specific response around several key words or ideas. Here are a few such key words or ideas:

M's: manpower, materials, methods, money, management
P's: purpose, program, policy, plan, procedure, practice, problems, pitfalls, personnel, public relations

a. Six basic steps in handling problems:
   1. Preliminary plan and background development
   2. Collect information, data and facts
   3. Analyze and interpret information, data and facts
   4. Analyze and develop solutions as well as make recommendations
   5. Prepare report and sell recommendations
   6. Install recommendations and follow up effectiveness

b. Pitfalls to avoid
   1. *Taking things for granted* – A statement of the situation does not necessarily imply that each of the elements is necessarily true; for example, a complaint may be invalid and biased so that all that can be taken for granted is that a complaint has been registered
   2. *Considering only one side of a situation* – Wherever possible, indicate several alternatives and then point out the reasons you selected the best one
   3. *Failing to indicate follow up* – Whenever your answer indicates action on your part, make certain that you will take proper follow-up action to see how successful your recommendations, procedures or actions turn out to be
   4. *Taking too long in answering any single question* – Remember to time your answers properly

IX. AFTER THE TEST

Scoring procedures differ in detail among civil service jurisdictions although the general principles are the same. Whether the papers are hand-scored or graded by machine we have described, they are nearly always graded by number. That is, the person who marks the paper knows only the number – never the name – of the applicant. Not until all the papers have been graded will they be matched with names. If other tests, such as training and experience or oral interview ratings have been given, scores will be combined. Different parts of the examination usually have different weights. For example, the written test might count 60 percent of the final grade, and a rating of training and experience 40 percent. In many jurisdictions, veterans will have a certain number of points added to their grades.

After the final grade has been determined, the names are placed in grade order and an eligible list is established. There are various methods for resolving ties between those who get the same final grade – probably the most common is to place first the name of the person whose application was received first. Job offers are made from the eligible list in the order the names appear on it. You will be notified of your grade and your rank as soon as all these computations have been made. This will be done as rapidly as possible.

People who are found to meet the requirements in the announcement are called "eligibles." Their names are put on a list of eligible candidates. An eligible's chances of getting a job depend on how high he stands on this list and how fast agencies are filling jobs from the list.

When a job is to be filled from a list of eligibles, the agency asks for the names of people on the list of eligibles for that job. When the civil service commission receives this request, it sends to the agency the names of the three people highest on this list. Or, if the job to be filled has specialized requirements, the office sends the agency the names of the top three persons who meet these requirements from the general list.

The appointing officer makes a choice from among the three people whose names were sent to him. If the selected person accepts the appointment, the names of the others are put back on the list to be considered for future openings.

That is the rule in hiring from all kinds of eligible lists, whether they are for typist, carpenter, chemist, or something else. For every vacancy, the appointing officer has his choice of any one of the top three eligibles on the list. This explains why the person whose name is on top of the list sometimes does not get an appointment when some of the persons lower on the list do. If the appointing officer chooses the second or third eligible, the No. 1 eligible does not get a job at once, but stays on the list until he is appointed or the list is terminated.

X. HOW TO PASS THE INTERVIEW TEST

The examination for which you applied requires an oral interview test. You have already taken the written test and you are now being called for the interview test – the final part of the formal examination.

You may think that it is not possible to prepare for an interview test and that there are no procedures to follow during an interview. Our purpose is to point out some things you can do in advance that will help you and some good rules to follow and pitfalls to avoid while you are being interviewed.

What is an interview supposed to test?

The written examination is designed to test the technical knowledge and competence of the candidate; the oral is designed to evaluate intangible qualities, not readily measured otherwise, and to establish a list showing the relative fitness of each candidate – as measured against his competitors – for the position sought. Scoring is not on the basis of "right" and "wrong," but on a sliding scale of values ranging from "not passable" to "outstanding." As a matter of fact, it is possible to achieve a relatively low score without a single "incorrect" answer because of evident weakness in the qualities being measured.

Occasionally, an examination may consist entirely of an oral test – either an individual or a group oral. In such cases, information is sought concerning the technical knowledges and abilities of the candidate, since there has been no written examination for this purpose. More commonly, however, an oral test is used to supplement a written examination.

Who conducts interviews?

The composition of oral boards varies among different jurisdictions. In nearly all, a representative of the personnel department serves as chairman. One of the members of the board may be a representative of the department in which the candidate would work. In some cases, "outside experts" are used, and, frequently, a businessman or some other representative of the general public is asked to serve. Labor and management or other special groups may be represented. The aim is to secure the services of experts in the appropriate field.

However the board is composed, it is a good idea (and not at all improper or unethical) to ascertain in advance of the interview who the members are and what groups they represent. When you are introduced to them, you will have some idea of their backgrounds and interests, and at least you will not stutter and stammer over their names.

What should be done before the interview?

While knowledge about the board members is useful and takes some of the surprise element out of the interview, there is other preparation which is more substantive. It *is* possible to prepare for an oral interview – in several ways:

1) Keep a copy of your application and review it carefully before the interview

This may be the only document before the oral board, and the starting point of the interview. Know what education and experience you have listed there, and the sequence and dates of all of it. Sometimes the board will ask you to review the highlights of your experience for them; you should not have to hem and haw doing it.

2) Study the class specification and the examination announcement

Usually, the oral board has one or both of these to guide them. The qualities, characteristics or knowledges required by the position sought are stated in these documents. They offer valuable clues as to the nature of the oral interview. For example, if the job involves supervisory responsibilities, the announcement will usually indicate that knowledge of modern supervisory methods and the qualifications of the candidate as a supervisor will be tested. If so, you can expect such questions, frequently in the form of a hypothetical situation which you are expected to solve. NEVER go into an oral without knowledge of the duties and responsibilities of the job you seek.

3) Think through each qualification required

Try to visualize the kind of questions you would ask if you were a board member. How well could you answer them? Try especially to appraise your own knowledge and background in each area, *measured against the job sought*, and identify any areas in which you are weak. Be critical and realistic – do not flatter yourself.

4) Do some general reading in areas in which you feel you may be weak

For example, if the job involves supervision and your past experience has NOT, some general reading in supervisory methods and practices, particularly in the field of human relations, might be useful. Do NOT study agency procedures or detailed manuals. The oral board will be testing your understanding and capacity, not your memory.

5) Get a good night's sleep and watch your general health and mental attitude

You will want a clear head at the interview. Take care of a cold or any other minor ailment, and of course, no hangovers.

What should be done on the day of the interview?

Now comes the day of the interview itself. Give yourself plenty of time to get there. Plan to arrive somewhat ahead of the scheduled time, particularly if your appointment is in the fore part of the day. If a previous candidate fails to appear, the board might be ready for you a bit early. By early afternoon an oral board is almost invariably behind schedule if there are many candidates, and you may have to wait. Take along a book or magazine to read, or your application to review, but leave any extraneous material in the waiting room when you go in for your interview. In any event, relax and compose yourself.

The matter of dress is important. The board is forming impressions about you – from your experience, your manners, your attitude, and your appearance. Give your personal appearance careful attention. Dress your best, but not your flashiest. Choose conservative, appropriate clothing, and be sure it is immaculate. This is a business interview, and your appearance should indicate that you regard it as such. Besides, being well groomed and properly dressed will help boost your confidence.

Sooner or later, someone will call your name and escort you into the interview room. *This is it.* From here on you are on your own. It is too late for any more preparation. But remember, you asked for this opportunity to prove your fitness, and you are here because your request was granted.

What happens when you go in?

The usual sequence of events will be as follows: The clerk (who is often the board stenographer) will introduce you to the chairman of the oral board, who will introduce you to the other members of the board. Acknowledge the introductions before you sit down. Do not be surprised if you find a microphone facing you or a stenotypist sitting by. Oral interviews are usually recorded in the event of an appeal or other review.

Usually the chairman of the board will open the interview by reviewing the highlights of your education and work experience from your application – primarily for the benefit of the other members of the board, as well as to get the material into the record. Do not interrupt or comment unless there is an error or significant misinterpretation; if that is the case, do not hesitate. But do not quibble about insignificant matters. Also, he will usually ask you some question about your education, experience or your present job – partly to get you to start talking and to establish the interviewing "rapport." He may start the actual questioning, or turn it over to one of the other members. Frequently, each member undertakes the questioning on a particular area, one in which he is perhaps most competent, so you can expect each member to participate in the examination. Because time is limited, you may also expect some rather abrupt switches in the direction the questioning takes, so do not be upset by it. Normally, a board member will not pursue a single line of questioning unless he discovers a particular strength or weakness.

After each member has participated, the chairman will usually ask whether any member has any further questions, then will ask you if you have anything you wish to add. Unless you are expecting this question, it may floor you. Worse, it may start you off on an extended, extemporaneous speech. The board is not usually seeking more information. The question is principally to offer you a last opportunity to present further qualifications or to indicate that you have nothing to add. So, if you feel that a significant qualification or characteristic has been overlooked, it is proper to point it out in a sentence or so. Do not compliment the board on the thoroughness of their examination – they have been sketchy, and you know it. If you wish, merely say, "No thank you, I have nothing further to add." This is a point where you can "talk yourself out" of a good impression or fail to present an important bit of information. Remember, *you close the interview yourself.*

The chairman will then say, "That is all, Mr. _____, thank you." Do not be startled; the interview is over, and quicker than you think. Thank him, gather your belongings and take your leave. Save your sigh of relief for the other side of the door.

How to put your best foot forward

Throughout this entire process, you may feel that the board individually and collectively is trying to pierce your defenses, seek out your hidden weaknesses and embarrass and confuse you. Actually, this is not true. They are obliged to make an appraisal of your qualifications for the job you are seeking, and they want to see you in your best light. Remember, they must interview all candidates and a non-cooperative candidate may become a failure in spite of their best efforts to bring out his qualifications. Here are 15 suggestions that will help you:

1) Be natural – Keep your attitude confident, not cocky

If you are not confident that you can do the job, do not expect the board to be. Do not apologize for your weaknesses, try to bring out your strong points. The board is interested in a positive, not negative, presentation. Cockiness will antagonize any board member and make him wonder if you are covering up a weakness by a false show of strength.

2) Get comfortable, but don't lounge or sprawl

Sit erectly but not stiffly. A careless posture may lead the board to conclude that you are careless in other things, or at least that you are not impressed by the importance of the occasion. Either conclusion is natural, even if incorrect. Do not fuss with your clothing, a pencil or an ashtray. Your hands may occasionally be useful to emphasize a point; do not let them become a point of distraction.

3) Do not wisecrack or make small talk

This is a serious situation, and your attitude should show that you consider it as such. Further, the time of the board is limited – they do not want to waste it, and neither should you.

4) Do not exaggerate your experience or abilities

In the first place, from information in the application or other interviews and sources, the board may know more about you than you think. Secondly, you probably will not get away with it. An experienced board is rather adept at spotting such a situation, so do not take the chance.

5) If you know a board member, do not make a point of it, yet do not hide it

Certainly you are not fooling him, and probably not the other members of the board. Do not try to take advantage of your acquaintanceship – it will probably do you little good.

6) Do not dominate the interview

Let the board do that. They will give you the clues – do not assume that you have to do all the talking. Realize that the board has a number of questions to ask you, and do not try to take up all the interview time by showing off your extensive knowledge of the answer to the first one.

7) Be attentive

You only have 20 minutes or so, and you should keep your attention at its sharpest throughout. When a member is addressing a problem or question to you, give him your undivided attention. Address your reply principally to him, but do not exclude the other board members.

8) Do not interrupt

A board member may be stating a problem for you to analyze. He will ask you a question when the time comes. Let him state the problem, and wait for the question.

9) Make sure you understand the question

Do not try to answer until you are sure what the question is. If it is not clear, restate it in your own words or ask the board member to clarify it for you. However, do not haggle about minor elements.

10) Reply promptly but not hastily

A common entry on oral board rating sheets is "candidate responded readily," or "candidate hesitated in replies." Respond as promptly and quickly as you can, but do not jump to a hasty, ill-considered answer.

11) Do not be peremptory in your answers

A brief answer is proper – but do not fire your answer back. That is a losing game from your point of view. The board member can probably ask questions much faster than you can answer them.

12) Do not try to create the answer you think the board member wants

He is interested in what kind of mind you have and how it works – not in playing games. Furthermore, he can usually spot this practice and will actually grade you down on it.

13) Do not switch sides in your reply merely to agree with a board member

Frequently, a member will take a contrary position merely to draw you out and to see if you are willing and able to defend your point of view. Do not start a debate, yet do not surrender a good position. If a position is worth taking, it is worth defending.

14) Do not be afraid to admit an error in judgment if you are shown to be wrong

The board knows that you are forced to reply without any opportunity for careful consideration. Your answer may be demonstrably wrong. If so, admit it and get on with the interview.

15) Do not dwell at length on your present job

The opening question may relate to your present assignment. Answer the question but do not go into an extended discussion. You are being examined for a *new* job, not your present one. As a matter of fact, try to phrase ALL your answers in terms of the job for which you are being examined.

Basis of Rating

Probably you will forget most of these "do's" and "don'ts" when you walk into the oral interview room. Even remembering them all will not ensure you a passing grade. Perhaps you did not have the qualifications in the first place. But remembering them will help you to put your best foot forward, without treading on the toes of the board members.

Rumor and popular opinion to the contrary notwithstanding, an oral board wants you to make the best appearance possible. They know you are under pressure – but they also want to see how you respond to it as a guide to what your reaction would be under the pressures of the job you seek. They will be influenced by the degree of poise you display, the personal traits you show and the manner in which you respond.

ABOUT THIS BOOK

This book contains tests divided into Examination Sections. Go through each test, answering every question in the margin. At the end of each test look at the answer key and check your answers. On the ones you got wrong, look at the right answer choice and learn. Do not fill in the answers first. Do not memorize the questions and answers, but understand the answer and principles involved. On your test, the questions will likely be different from the samples. Questions are changed and new ones added. If you understand these past questions you should have success with any changes that arise. Tests may consist of several types of questions. We have additional books on each subject should more study be advisable or necessary for you. Finally, the more you study, the better prepared you will be. This book is intended to be the last thing you study before you walk into the examination room. Prior study of relevant texts is also recommended. NLC publishes some of these in our Fundamental Series. Knowledge and good sense are important factors in passing your exam. Good luck also helps. So now study this Passbook, absorb the material contained within and take that knowledge into the examination. Then do your best to pass that exam.

EXAMINATION SECTION

EXAMINATION SECTION
TEST 1

DIRECTIONS: Each question or incomplete statement is followed by several suggested answers or completions. Select the one that BEST answers the question or completes the statement. *PRINT THE LETTER OF THE CORRECT ANSWER IN THE SPACE AT THE RIGHT.*

1. A maintenance man complains to you that he is getting all the boring jobs to do. You check and find that his complaint has no basis in fact.
The one of the following which is the MOST likely reason why the maintenance man made such a claim is that he

    A. wants to get even with the supervisor
    B. lives in a world of fantasy
    C. believes the injustice to be real
    D. is jealous of other workers

1.____

2. When on preliminary review of a mechanic's written grievance you feel the grievance to be unfounded, the FIRST step you should take is to

    A. show the mechanic where he is wrong
    B. check carefully to find out why the mechanic thinks that way
    C. try to humor the mechanic out of it
    D. tell the mechanic to stop complaining

2.____

3. Assume that you decide to hold a private meeting with one of your mechanics who has a drinking problem that is affecting his work.
At the meeting, the BEST way for you to handle this situation is to

    A. tell the mechanic off and then listen to what he has to say
    B. criticize the mechanic's behavior to get him to *open up* in order to help him correct his problem quickly
    C. try to get the mechanic to recognize his problem and find ways to solve it
    D. limit the discussion to matters concerning only the problem and look for immediate results

3.____

4. The one of the following which is a generally accepted guide in criticizing a subordinate EFFECTIVELY is to

    A. criticize the improper act, not the individual
    B. put the listener on the defensive
    C. make the criticism general instead of specific
    D. correct the personality, not the situation

4.____

5. The one of the following disciplinary methods by which you are MOST likely to be successful in getting a problem employee to improve his behavior is when you

    A. discipline the employee in front of others
    B. consider the matter to be ended after the disciplining
    C. give the exact same discipline no matter how serious the wrongdoing
    D. make an example of the employee

5.____

6. Of the following statements, the one that is MOST applicable to a disciplinary situation is   6.____
   that discipline should be

   A. used after a cooling-off period
   B. identical for all employees
   C. consistent with the violation
   D. based on personal feelings

7. The one of the following approaches that is MOST important for you to take in evaluating   7.____
   a mechanic in order to increase his work productivity is to

   A. first have him evaluate his own performance
   B. meet with him to discuss how he is doing and what is expected on the job
   C. send him a copy of your evaluation of his work performance and give him the
      opportunity to submit written comments
   D. express in writing your appreciation of his work

8. Assume that you say to one of the mechanics, *Jim, that job you turned out today was*   8.____
   top-notch. I didn't think you could do so well with the kind of material you had to work
   with.
   This statement BEST describes an example of your

   A. recognition of the man's work
   B. disrespect for the man's feelings
   C. personal favoritism of the man
   D. constructive criticism of the man's work

9. In general, the OUTSTANDING characteristic of employees over 50 years of age is their   9.____
   A. resistance   B. endurance
   C. wisdom   D. job stability

10. You should be interested in the morale of your men because morale is MOST often asso-   10.____
    ciated with

    A. mechanization   B. automation
    C. production   D. seniority regulations

11. Assume that the maintenance work order system is about to be changed. Your workers   11.____
    would MOST likely show the LEAST resistance to this change if you

    A. downgrade the old maintenance work order system
    B. tell your workers how the change will benefit them
    C. post the notice of the change on the bulletin board
    D. tell the workers how the change will benefit management

12. Of the following, the BEST way to motivate a newly appointed mechanic is to   12.____

    A. explain the meaning of each assignment
    B. make the work more physically demanding
    C. test the mechanic's ability
    D. use as much authority as possible

13. The one of the following which is the LEAST important reason for giving employees information concerning policy changes which will affect them is that employees should know   13._____

   A. why the change is being made
   B. who will be affected by the change
   C. when the change will go into effect
   D. how much savings will be made by the change

14. A foreman who knows how to handle his men will MOST likely get them to produce more by treating them   14._____

   A. alike   B. as individuals
   C. on a casual basis   D. as a group

15. Of the following items, the one that a supervisor has the MOST right to expect from his employees is   15._____

   A. liking the job
   B. a fair day's work
   C. equal skill of all mechanics
   D. perfection

16. The one of the following which is the BEST practice for you to follow in handling a dispute between the workers is to   16._____

   A. side with one of the workers so as to end the dispute quickly
   B. pay no attention to the dispute and let the workers settle it themselves
   C. listen to each worker's story of the dispute and then decide how to settle it
   D. discuss the dispute with other workers and then decide how to settle it

17. You are likely to run into an employee morale problem when assigning a dirty job that comes up often.
   Of the following, the BEST method of assigning this work is to   17._____

   A. rotate this assignment
   B. assign it to the fastest worker
   C. assign it by seniority
   D. assign it to the least skilled worker

18. Of the following, the one that is generally regarded as the BEST aid to high work productivity of subordinates is a supervisor's skill in   18._____

   A. record keeping
   B. technical work
   C. setting up rules and regulations
   D. human relations

19. The BEST way to help a mechanic who comes to you for advice on a personal problem is to   19._____

   A. listen to the worker's problem without passing judgment
   B. tell the worker to forget about the problem and to stop letting it interfere with his work
   C. talk about your own personal problems to the worker
   D. mind your own business and leave the worker alone

20. You are in charge of the maintenance shop and have learned that within the next two weeks the maintenance shop will be moved to a new location on the plant grounds, but you have not learned why this move is taking place. Assume that you have decided not to keep this information from your mechanics until the reason is known but to inform them of this matter now.
Of the following, which one is the BEST argument that can be made regarding your decision?

    A. *Acceptable;* because although the reason is not now known, the mechanics will eventually find out about the move
    B. *Unacceptable;* because the mechanics do not know at this time the reason for the move and this will cause anxiety on their part
    C. *Acceptable;* because the mechanics will be affected by the move and they should be told what is happening
    D. *Unacceptable;* because the mechanics' advance knowledge of the move will tend to slow down their work output

20.____

21. Of the following, the FIRST action for a foreman to take in making a decision is to

    A. get all the facts
    B. develop alternate solutions
    C. get opinions of others
    D. know the results in advance

21.____

22. Assume that you have just been promoted to foreman.
Of the following, the BEST practice to follow regarding your previous experience at the mechanic's level is to

    A. continue to fraternize with your old friends
    B. use this experience to better understand those who now work for you
    C. use your old connections to keep top management informed of mechanics' views
    D. forget the mechanics' points of view

22.____

23. You have decided to hold regular group discussions with your subordinates on various aspects of their duties.
Of the following methods you might use to begin such a program, the one which is likely to be MOST productive is to

    A. express your own ideas and persuade the group to accept them
    B. save time and cover more ground by asking questions calling for yes or no answers
    C. propose to the group a general plan of action rather than specific ideas carefully worked out
    D. provide an informal atmosphere for the exchange of ideas

23.____

24. The principle of learning by which a foreman might get the BEST results in training his subordinates is:

    A. Letting the learner discover and correct his own mistakes
    B. Teaching the most technical part of the work first
    C. Teaching all parts of the work during the first training session
    D. Getting the learner to use as many of his five senses as possible

24.____

25. A new mechanic is to be trained to do an involved operation containing several steps of   25.____
varying difficulty. This mechanic will MOST likely learn the operation more quickly if he is
taught

    A. each step in its proper order
    B. the hardest steps first
    C. the easiest steps first
    D. first the steps that do not require tools

_____

KEY (CORRECT ANSWERS)

1.	C		11.	B
2.	B		12.	A
3.	C		13.	D
4.	A		14.	B
5.	B		15.	B
6.	C		16.	C
7.	B		17.	A
8.	A		18.	D
9.	D		19.	A
10.	C		20.	C

21.	A
22.	B
23.	D
24.	D
25.	C

_____

TEST 2

DIRECTIONS: Each question or incomplete statement is followed by several suggested answers or completions. Select the one that BEST answers the question or completes the statement. *PRINT THE LETTER OF THE CORRECT ANSWER IN THE SPACE AT THE RIGHT.*

1. The one of the following job situations in which it is better to give a written order than an oral order is when

   A. the job involves many details
   B. you can check the job's progress easily
   C. the job is repetitive in nature
   D. there is an emergency

   1.____

2. Which one of the following serves as the BEST guideline for you to follow for effective written reports?
   Keep sentences

   A. short and limit sentences to one thought
   B. short and use as many thoughts as possible
   C. long and limit sentences to one thought
   D. long and use as many thoughts as possible

   2.____

3. Of the following, the BEST reason why a foreman generally should not do the work of an individual mechanic is that

   A. the shop's production figures will not be accurate
   B. a foreman is paid to supervise
   C. the foreman must maintain his authority
   D. the employee may become self-conscious

   3.____

4. One method by which a foreman might prepare written reports to management is to begin with the conclusions, results, or summary and to follow this with the supporting data.
   The BEST reason why management may prefer this form of report is because

   A. management lacks the specific training to understand the data
   B. the data completely supports the conclusions
   C. time is saved by getting to the conclusions of the report first
   D. the data contains all the information that is required for making the conclusions

   4.____

5. Forms used for time records and work orders are important to the work of a foreman PRIMARILY because they give him

   A. the knowledge of and familiarity with work operations
   B. the means of control of personnel, material, or job costs
   C. the means for communicating with other workers
   D. a useful method for making filing procedures easier

   5.____

6. The one of the following which is the MOST important factor in determining the number   6.____
of employees you can effectively supervise is the

    A. type of work to be performed
    B. priority of the work to be performed
    C. salary level of the workers
    D. ratio of permanent employees to temporary employees

7. Of the following, you will be MOST productive in carrying out your supervisory responsi-   7.____
bilities if you

    A. are capable of doing the same work as your mechanics
    B. meet with your mechanics frequently
    C. are very friendly with your mechanics
    D. get work done through your mechanics

8. You have been asked to prepare the annual budget for your maintenance shop.   8.____
The one of the following which is the FIRST step you should take in preparing this budget is to determine the

    A. amount of maintenance work which is scheduled for the shop
    B. time it takes for a specific unit of work to be completed
    C. current workload of each employee in the shop
    D. policies and procedures of the shop's operations

9. When determining the amount of work you expect a group of mechanics to perform in a   9.____
given time, the BEST procedure for you to follow should be to

    A. aim for a higher level of production than that of the most productive worker
    B. stay at the present production level
    C. set general instead of specific goals
    D. let workers participate in the determination whenever possible

10. You have been asked to set next year's performance goals concerning the ratio of jobs   10.____
completed on schedule to total jobs worked. A review of last year's record shows that the
workers completed their jobs on schedule 85% of the time, with the best ones showing
an on-time ratio of 92% and the poorest ones showing an on-time ratio of 65%.
Using these facts in line with generally accepted goal-setting practices, you should set
a performance ratio for the next year on the basis of _____ average with a _____
minimum acceptable for any employee.

    A. 85%; 65%   B. 85%; 70%   C. 90%; 65%   D. 90%; 70%

11. It is important for you to be able to identify the critical parts of a large project such as the   11.____
remodeling of your maintenance shop.
The one of the following which is the BEST reason why this is important is that it may

    A. help you to set up good communications between you and your workers
    B. give you a better understanding of the purpose of the project
    C. give you control over the time and cost involved in the project
    D. help you to determine who are your most productive workers

12. When doing work planning for your shop, the factor that you should normally consider   12._____
LAST among the following is knowing your

    A. major objectives   B. record keeping system
    C. minor objectives   D. priorities

13. You have the responsibility for ordering all materials for your maintenance shop. A listing   13._____
of materials needed for the operations of your shop is long overdue. You realize that you
are unable to find time to take care of the inventory personally because of a high priority
project you have been working on which has been taking all of your time. You do not
know when you will be finished with the project.
The BEST of the following courses of action to take in handling this inventory matter is
to

    A. request that you be taken off the project immediately so that you may take care of
        the inventory
    B. complete your high priority project and then do the inventory yourself
    C. volunteer to work overtime so that you may complete the inventory while continuing
        with the project
    D. assign the inventory work to a competent subordinate

14. You have the authority and responsibility for seeing that proper records are kept in your   14._____
shop. Assume that you decide to delegate to a records clerk the responsibility for collect-
ing the time sheets and the authority to make changes on the time sheets to correct the
information when necessary.
Of the following, which one is the BEST argument that can be made regarding your
decision?

    A. *Unacceptable*; because you can delegate only your responsibility but none of your
        authority to the records clerk
    B. *Acceptable*; because you can delegate some of your authority and some of your
        responsibility to the records clerk
    C. *Unacceptable;* because you can delegate only your authority but none of your
        responsibility to the records clerk
    D. *Acceptable;* because you can delegate all your responsibility and all your authority
        to the records clerk

15. You will LEAST likely be able to do an effective job of controlling operating costs if you   15._____

    A. eliminate idle time   B. reduce absenteeism
    C. raise your budget   D. combine work operations

16. Of the following actions, the one which is LEAST likely to help in carrying out your   16._____
responsibilities of looking after the interests of your workers is to

    A. crack down on your workers when necessary
    B. let your workers know that you support company policy
    C. prevent the transfers of your workers
    D. back up your workers in a controversy

17. The term *accountability*, as used in management of supervision, means MOST NEARLY   17._____

    A. responsibility for results   B. record keeping
    C. bookkeeping systems   D. inventory control

18. Assume that you have been unable to convince an employee of the seriousness of his poor attendance record by talking to him.
The one of the following which is the BEST course of action for you to take is to

    A. keep talking to the employee
    B. recommend that a written warning be given
    C. consider transferring the employee to another work location
    D. recommend that the employee be fired

18.____

19. When delegating work to a subordinate foreman, you should NOT

    A. delegate the right to make any decisions
    B. be interested in the results of the work, but in the method of doing the work
    C. delegate any work that you can do better than your subordinate
    D. give up your final responsibility for the work

19.____

20. Of the following statements, the BEST reason why proper scheduling of maintenance work is important is that it

    A. eliminates the need for individual job work orders
    B. classifies job skills in accordance with performance
    C. minimizes lost time in performing any maintenance job
    D. determines needed repairs in various locations

20.____

21. Of the following factors, the one which is of LEAST importance in determining the number of subordinates that an individual should be assigned to supervise is the

    A. nature of the work being supervised
    B. qualifications of the individual as a supervisor
    C. capabilities of the subordinates
    D. lines of promotion for the subordinates

21.____

22. Suppose that a large number of semi-literate residents of this city have been requesting the assistance of your department. You are asked to prepare a form which these applicants will be required to fill out before their requests will be considered.
In view of these facts, the one of the following factors to which you should give the GREATEST amount of consideration in preparing this form is the

    A. size of the form
    B. sequence of the information asked for on the form
    C. level of difficulty of the language used in the form
    D. number of times which the form will have to be reviewed

22.____

23. A budget is a plan whereby a goal is set for future operations. It affords a medium for comparing actual expenditures with planned expenditures.
The one of the following which is the MOST accurate statement on the basis of this statement is that

    A. the budget serves as an accurate measure of past as well as future expenditures
    B. the budget presents an estimate of expenditures to be made in the future
    C. budget estimates should be based upon past budget requirements
    D. planned expenditures usually fall short of actual expenditures

23.____

24. A foreman who is familiar with modern management principles should know that the one   24.____
of the following requirements of an administrator which is LEAST important is his ability
to

   A. coordinate work
   B. plan, organize, and direct the work under his control
   C. cooperate with others
   D. perform the duties of the employees under his jurisdiction

25. The one of the following which should be considered the LEAST important objective of   25.____
the service rating system is to

   A. rate the employees on the basis of their potential abilities
   B. establish a basis for assigning employees to special types of work
   C. provide a means of recognizing superior work performance
   D. reveal the need for training as well as the effectiveness of a training program

---

KEY (CORRECT ANSWERS)

1. A		11. C
2. A		12. B
3. B		13. D
4. C		14. B
5. B		15. C
6. A		16. C
7. D		17. A
8. A		18. B
9. D		19. D
10. D		20. C

21. D
22. C
23. B
24. D
25. A

EXAMINATION SECTION
TEST 1

DIRECTIONS: Each question or incomplete statement is followed by several suggested answers or completions. Select the one that BEST answers the question or completes the statement. *PRINT THE LETTER OF THE CORRECT ANSWER IN THE SPACE AT THE RIGHT.*

1. Front stabilizer bars on automotive vehicles are set in such a manner that they   1.____

    A.   apply force opposite to that of the springs when the springs are deflected equally
    B.   normally connect to both lower control arms
    C.   are adjustable in order to level the vehicle
    D.   have one end attached to the lower control arm and the other end attached to the frame

2. Ignition point contact alignment is BEST adjusted by bending the   2.____

    A.   movable point arm   B.   pivot post
    C.   breaker plate   D.   stationary point bracket

3. When disc brake pads are retracted so as not to be touching the braking disc, the amount of retraction   3.____

    A.   is affected by the piston return springs
    B.   must be a minimum of 1/32 of an inch
    C.   is affected by the piston seals
    D.   is limited by the metering valve

4. A PROPERLY operating positive crankcase ventilation valve will   4.____

    A.   control air flow as a direct function of engine speed
    B.   increase air flow in direct proportion to the increase in manifold vacuum
    C.   shut off air flow at high intake manifold vacuum
    D.   reduce air flow at high intake manifold vacuum

5. The air-fuel ratio, by weight, in a properly functioning gasoline automotive engine is MOST NEARLY   5.____

    A.   15:1   B.   30:1   C.   600:1   D.   9000:1

6. Cam ground pistons are distinguished by   6.____

    A.   being ground perfectly round
    B.   having a larger diameter across the piston pin faces
    C.   having a larger diameter parallel to the crankshaft centerline
    D.   having a larger diameter perpendicular to the crankshaft centerline

7. In an automotive engine, the intake valves USUALLY open _____ TDC and close _____ BDC of the intake stroke.   7.____

    A.   after; after   B.   after; before
    C.   before; before   D.   before; after

8. In an automotive engine, the exhaust valves USUALLY open _____ BDC of the power stroke and _____ TDC of the intake stroke.　　8._____

   A. after; before   B. before; before
   C. before; after   D. after; after

9. The PRIMARY function of a blower on a two-cycle diesel engine is to　　9._____

   A. provide air for scavenging
   B. increase the compression ratio
   C. blow in the fuel-air mixture
   D. cool the oil after compression in the injector pump

10. Excessive free travel of the clutch pedal would be indicated if the　　10._____

   A. transmission was hard to shift smoothly
   B. clutch slipped when fully engaged
   C. throwout bearing failed prematurely
   D. release levers were worn

11. Vacuum is usually referred to in inches of mercury.
The number of pounds per square inch pressure above zero (absolute pressure) of a 20 inch vacuum is MOST NEARLY　　11._____

   A. 4.9   B. 7.4   C. 9.6   D. 11.8

12. Only a portion of the heat energy released by the gasoline in an automotive engine is transmitted to the wheels for driving purposes.
In an automobile in good condition and with an efficiently operating engine, this portion is MOST NEARLY　　12._____

   A. 90%   B. 50%   C. 20%   D. 2%

13. An adjustment is made to the right front wheel of a vehicle equipped with shims at the junction of the upper suspension arm and the frame support by moving the upper suspension arm away from the frame a greater amount in the front than in the rear.
This is done to　　13._____

   A. increase the steering knuckle angle
   B. adjust the caster in a negative direction
   C. adjust the camber in a negative direction
   D. adjust the caster in a rotary direction

14. In an automotive rear axle in which the pinion gear engages the ring gear below the centerline of the axle, the cut of the pinion and ring gear is　　14._____

   A. spiral bevel   B. spur bevel
   C. double helical   D. hypoid

15. Of the following statements concerning the operation in low gear of a fully synchronized (in forward gears) three-speed transmission, the one that is NOT correct is that　　15._____

   A. both clutch sleeves must engage gears
   B. power is being transmitted through the countershaft gears
   C. one clutch sleeve must be engaged
   D. the reverse idler gear is being driven by a countershaft gear

Questions 16-17.

DIRECTIONS: Questions 16 and 17 are to be answered in accordance with the following paragraph.

Steam cleaners get their name from the fact that steam is used to generate pressure and is also a by-product of heating the cleaning solution. Steam itself has little cleaning power. It will melt some soils, but it does not dissolve them, break them up, or destroy their clinging power. Rather surprisingly, good machines generate as little steam as possible. Modern surface chemistry depends on a chemical solution to dissolve dirt, destroy its clinging power, and hold it in suspension. Steam actually hinders such a solution, but heat helps its physical and chemical action. Cleaning is most efficient when a hot solution reaches the work in heavy volume.

16. In accordance with the above paragraph, for MOST efficient cleaning,   16._____

    A. a heavy volume of steam is needed
    B. hot steam is needed to break up the soils
    C. steam is used to dissolve the surface dirt
    D. a hot chemical solution should always be used

17. With reference to the above paragraph, the steam in a steam cleaner is used to   17._____

    A. generate pressure
    B. create by-product chemicals
    C. slow down the chemical action of the cleaning solution
    D. dissolve accumulations of dirt

18. An electromechanical regulator for an automotive alternator differs from a DC generator   18._____
in that the alternator regulator

    A. has a current regulator unit
    B. has a reverse current relay
    C. does not have a current regulator unit
    D. does not have a voltage regulator unit

19. Of the following statements concerning the charging of lead acid batteries, the one   19._____
MOST NEARLY correct is that

    A. a fast charge (40-50 amp, 12V) can safely be used if the battery temperature does not exceed 185° F
    B. heavily sulphated batteries respond best to a slow charging rate
    C. a battery on trickle charge cannot be damaged by overcharging
    D. the higher the battery temperature, the smaller the charging current with constant applied voltage

20. The ignition points of a conventional ignition system are adjusted to increase the point   20._____
gap.
This adjustment will

    A. increase the dwell angle
    B. retard the ignition timing

    C. advance the ignition timing
    D. decrease the dwell angle with no change in ignition timing

21. A single diaphragm distributor vacuum advance unit   21.____

    A. advances the spark under part throttle operation
    B. is connected to the intake manifold
    C. advances the spark in proportion to engine speed
    D. advances the spark during acceleration or full throttle operation

22. The part of a conventional ignition system that could properly be considered part of 22.____
BOTH the primary and secondary circuits would be the

    A. condenser   B. distributor rotor
    C. coil   D. ignition points

23. As compared to a conventional type of spark plug, a resistor type of spark plug will 23.____

    A. reduce the inductive portion of the spark
    B. lengthen the capacitive portion of the spark
    C. require a higher voltage to function properly
    D. have an auxiliary air gap

24. If the criterion that limits the yearly major repair expenses to 30% of the current value of 24.____
equipment were reduced to 15% and the depreciation rate of 20% of original cost each
year were increased to 25%, the expenses for major repairs in a shop handling a constant flow of equipment of the same type and age would

    A. decrease   B. remain the same
    C. increase slightly   D. increase markedly

Question 25.

DIRECTIONS: Question 25 is to be answered in accordance with the following paragraph.

*The storage battery is a lead-acid, electrochemical device used for storing energy in its
chemical form. The battery does not actually store electricity, but converts an electrical
charge into chemical energy which is stored until the battery terminals are connected to a
closed external circuit. When the circuit is closed, the chemical energy inside the battery is
transformed back into electrical energy through a chemical action, and, as a result, current
flows through the circuit.*

25. According to the above paragraph, a lead-acid battery stores   25.____

    A. current   B. electricity
    C. electrical energy   D. chemical energy

26. A cam is to be fashioned from a circular disc with a hole drilled eccentrically on a diame- 26.____
ter of the disc but perpendicularly to the surface of the disc. A keyed shaft is to be fitted
into the hole so that the disc may be rotated in order to function as a cam.
If the disc is 5 inches in diameter and 1/2 inch thick and the hole is to be 1 inch in
diameter, the distance from the center of the disc to the center of the hole to be drilled
in order for the disc to act as a cam with a 2 inch lift should be _____ inch(es).

    A. 2   B. 1 1/2   C. 1   D. 1/2

27. Sparks and open flames should be kept away from batteries that are being charged   27.____
because of the danger of explosion or fire resulting from the ignition of the generated
_____ gas.

    A. fluorine   B. nitrogen   C. hydrogen   D. argon

28. Safety standards indicate that the use of any motor vehicle equipment having an   28.____
obstructed view to the rear

    A. requires a reverse signal alarm audible above the surrounding noise level
    B. requires the use of two back-up lights of at least 45 watt capacity each
    C. requires the use of a safety contact alarm rear bumper audible above the surround-
        ing noise level
    D. is prohibited

29. In the performance of a compression test, it is found that the addition of a tablespoon of   29.____
SAE 40 motor oil causes no significant increase in the low compression pressure.
The low compression pressure is most probably NOT caused by

    A. a broken piston   B. a leaking head gasket
    C. sticking valves   D. worn piston rings

30. Automotive exhaust gas analyzers, as generally used in emission control maintenance,   30.____
will NORMALLY indicate the percentage of

    A. NO   B. SO_2 C. CO_2 D. CO

Questions 31-33.

DIRECTIONS: Questions 31 through 33 are to be answered in accordance with the information given below.

*For most efficient utilization of funds and facilities, the rule has been established that the
repair cost of a part cannot exceed 50% of the vendor's price for a new part and that a part
cannot be made in-house if the cost would be more than 70% of the vendor's price for a new
one.*

*You have found that the average removed sprocket shaft, as shown below, requires both
bearing sections to be built up and remachined and one sprocket section to be built up and
remachined. The foreman of the machine shop has given you the following information relative to the manufacture or repair of the shafts:*

	Time	*Rate*
Weld 1 bearing section	*1.2 hours*	*$8/hr.*
Weld 1 keyway and sprocket section	*2.0 hours*	*$8/hr.*
Turn 1 bearing section	*0.6 hours*	*$8/hr.*
Turn 1 sprocket section	*0.7 hours*	*$8/hr.*
Cut 1 keyway	*0.5 hours*	*$8/hr.*

Purchasing has quoted shaft material at $12/ft. and new shafts at $160 each.

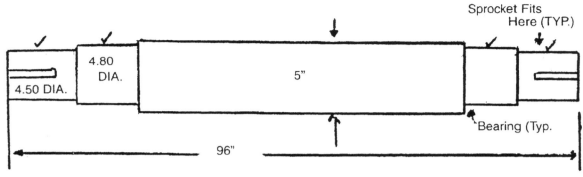

31. In accordance with the information given above, the cost for in-house manufacture of one 31._____
    shaft is

    A. $110.40   B. $112.00   C. $124.80   D. $132.60

32. In accordance with the information given above, the cost of in-house repair of one shaft 32._____
    is

    A. $68.40   B. $54.40   C. $30.40   D. $14.40

33. In accordance with the information given above, the PROPER procedure to follow, under 33._____
    the given rules, is to

    A. repair old shafts and buy new shafts
    B. repair old shafts and make new shafts
    C. make no repairs but make new shafts
    D. make no repairs but buy new shafts

34. The series of small vertical oscillations in the area of the center of a superimposed pat- 34._____
    tern on the screen of a properly adjusted oscilloscope showing the secondary circuit of a
    properly tuned automotive engine directly follows the instant at which the

    A. spark plugs fire   B. points open
    C. points close   D. coil starts to discharge

35. A rectangularly shaped repair facility for light trucks is 160 feet wide and 260 feet long. A 35._____
    10 foot space is provided along each wall for benches and equipment. A 60 foot wide
    area in the middle of the floor is to remain clear for its entire 260 foot length. The
    entrance to the shop is at one end of this open area. Assuming that there are no columns
    to contend with, the MAXIMUM area available for parking of trucks is _____ square
    feet.

    A. 15,600   B. 19,200   C. 26,000   D. 41,600

36. A criterion is established that limits the yearly major repair expenses to 30% of the cur- 36._____
    rent value of the equipment. Equipment is depreciated at a rate of 20% of its original cost
    each year. A truck purchased on January 1, 2000 for $9,000 had a reconditioned engine
    installed in February 2003 at a total cost of $900.
    The amount of money available for additional major repairs on this truck in 2003 was

    A. none   B. $180   C. $360   D. $720

37. Twenty fuel injectors are ordered for your shop by the purchasing department. The terms are list, less 30%, less 10%, less 5%.
If the list price of a fuel injector is $70 and all terms are met upon delivery, the charges to your budget will be

    A. $1359.60   B. $1085.40   C. $837.90   D. $630.80

    7.____

38. The cylinders of an 8 cylinder automotive engine have a bore of 4 inches and the pistons have a stroke of 4 inches. If the clearance volume in each cylinder is 6.0 cubic inches, the cubic inch displacement of the engine is MOST NEARLY

    A. 306   B. 354   C. 402   D. 450

    38.____

39. An automotive engine cylinder has a bore of 4 inches and its pistons have a stroke of 4 inches.
If the clearance volume in the cylinder is 6.0 cubic inches, the compression ratio is MOST NEARLY

    A. 10.62:1   B. 9.37:1   C. 8.37:1   D. 7.62:1

    39.____

40. Of the following deficiencies found during the inspection of passenger car brakes for issuance of a State Certificate of Inspection, the one that would be cause for REJEC-TION of the car brakes is that

    A. there is less than 3/64 in. of lining remaining above the drum brake shoe lining rivet heads
    B. the master cylinder brake fluid level is anything less than full
    C. the brake drums have been found to be more than .020 inches oversize
    D. the brake pedal reserve is less than one-half the total possible travel

    40.____

41. When checking a fuel pump for proper operation, it is ALWAYS necessary to

    A. connect a vacuum gage to the fuel line between the pump and the carburetor
    B. make the vacuum test before the pressure test
    C. set the gages at floor level to maintain a consistent reference point
    D. make a vacuum test if the pressure or volume test results are not up to specification

    41.____

42. On a single cylinder 4 stroke cycle internal combustion engine equipped with a flywheel magneto, the ignition points open at the end of the _____ strokes.

    A. intake and the compression
    B. compression and the exhaust
    C. power and the compression
    D. intake and the power

    42.____

43. An impulse coupling is MOST usually found in

    A. an automatic transmission
    B. a limited slip differential
    C. the front axle of 4 wheel drive vehicles
    D. a magneto

    43.____

Questions 44-45.

DIRECTIONS: Questions 44 and 45 are to be answered in accordance with the following paragraph.

You have been instructed to expedite the fabrication of four special salt spreader trucks using chassis that are available in the shop. All four trucks must be delivered before the opening of business on December 1, 2015. Based on workload and available hours, the fore-man of the body shop indicates that he could manufacture one complete salt spreader body in five weeks, with one additional week required for mounting and securing each body to the available chassis. No work could begin on the body until the engines and hydraulic compo-nents, which would have to be purchased, were available for use. The purchasing depart-ment has promised delivery of engines and hydraulic components three months after the order is placed. (Assume that all months have four weeks and the same crew is doing the assembling and manufacturing.)

44. With reference to the above paragraph, assuming that the purchasing department placed the order at the beginning of the first week in February 2015 and ultimate delivery of the engines and components was delayed by six weeks, the date of completion of the first salt spreader truckwould be CLOSEST to the end of the _____ week in _____, 2015.   44._____

   A. fourth; July   B. second; August
   C. fourth; August   D. first; September

45. With reference to the above paragraph, the LATEST date that the engines and associ-ated hydraulic components could be requisitioned in order to meet the specified deadline would be CLOSEST to the beginning of the _____ week in _____, 2015.   45._____

   A. first; February   B. first; March
   C. third; March   D. first; April

46. In an OHV internal combustion engine, excessive inlet valve guide clearance manifests itself initially by   46._____

   A. lowered cylinder compression pressure
   B. excessive oil consumption
   C. increased manifold vacuum
   D. fluffy black deposits on spark plugs

47. One of your mechanics has performed an automotive fuel system test and reports a fuel flow of 1/2 pint/minute at 500 rpm, a static fuel pump discharge pressure of 6 psi, and a 15 in.Hg vacuum at the pump inlet flex line.
These results should suggest to the mechanic that   47._____

   A. the system was operating properly
   B. he should check for a leaking pump inlet flex line
   C. he should replace the defective fuel pump
   D. check for a plugged inlet fuel line

48. An electrician is wiring a light switch on a light truck. The light switch will operate the following lamp bulbs: 48.____

Quantity	No.	Description	Current (each)
2	194	Marker	.3
3	67	Clearance	.4
2	1157	Stop/tail	2.1/ .6
2	1141	Front park	1.5
2	6012	Headlamp	4.2/3.4

The parking lamps are to be on when the headlamps are on.
If the permissible current capacities of wire are

    16 gage   0 - 6 amp
    14 gage   6 - 15 amp
    12 gage   15 - 20 amp
    10 gage   20 - 25 amp

the smallest size wire that the electrician should use to supply power to the switch would be a _____ gage wire.

A. 16   B. 14   C. 12   D. 10

49. In an automotive cooling system, the bypass passage or bypass valve   49.____

   A. permits a small amount of coolant to pass around the thermostat to maintain circulation
   B. permits the circulation of coolant through the engine block when the thermostat is closed
   C. directly connects the pump inlet to the pump discharge to prevent cavitation in the pump
   D. prevents the coolant in the system from developing excessive pressure

50. When adjusting a recirculating ball worm-and-nut steering gear, it is IMPROPER procedure to   50.____

   A. remove the pitman arm before making adjustments
   B. loosen the lash adjustment before checking bearing preload
   C. make the pitman shaft gear over center adjustment with the steering wheel in the center of travel position
   D. adjust the bearing preload with the steering wheel in the center of travel position

——————

KEY (CORRECT ANSWERS)

1.	B	11.	A	21.	A	31.	C	41.	D
2.	D	12.	C	22.	C	32.	B	42.	B
3.	C	13.	B	23.	A	33.	A	43.	D
4.	D	14.	D	24.	A	34.	C	44.	A
5.	A	15.	A	25.	D	35.	B	45.	B
6.	D	16.	D	26.	C	36.	B	46.	B
7.	D	17.	A	27.	C	37.	C	47.	D
8.	C	18.	C	28.	A	38.	C	48.	B
9.	A	19.	B	29.	D	39.	B	49.	B
10.	A	20.	C	30.	D	40.	B	50.	D

EXAMINATION SECTION
TEST 1

DIRECTIONS: Each question or incomplete statement is followed by several suggested answers or completions. Select the one that BEST answers the question or completes the statement. *PRINT THE LETTER OF THE CORRECT ANSWER IN THE SPACE AT THE RIGHT.*

1. Of the following procedures by which a foreman may train his assistant to take his place during his absence, the one most generally acceptable as the BEST is for the foreman to

    1.____

    A. guide the assistant in actually carrying out all the important procedures involved in the work he will have to do
    B. have the assistant attend group meetings and ask questions
    C. explain carefully to the assistant all the procedures involved, having him practice these procedures in the actual situation when the foreman is away
    D. put the assistant in charge of the unit for a few days to let him learn by actual practice

2. Assume that you are a foreman and you assign one of your hardest working men to do some paper work which he has never done before. Because of his inexperience, he makes many errors.
Of the following, the MOST advisable course of action for you to take is to

    2.____

    A. express your appreciation for his willingness and show him how to do the work better
    B. praise his effort but reprimand him for his performance
    C. praise his work to show appreciation of his efforts
    D. say nothing but do not assign him to that work again

3. Assume that you are a foreman and a man under your supervision, who is very efficient, is constantly complaining about the type of work assigned to him. You have noticed that his complaints have a bad effect on the other men. Of the following, the BEST course of action for you to take in this situation is to

    3.____

    A. ask the men to try to overlook his faults
    B. determine the cause of his attitude and try to make an adjustment in his work assignment
    C. secure his transfer to another shop or unit being supervised by a different foreman
    D. let the man make his own work assignments

4. Of the following, the MOST important reason for operating within a budget is that a budget will

    4.____

    A. permit a department or agency to cut down on provisional appointments
    B. control spending in advance
    C. explain the area of responsibility of a department or agency
    D. set up a good base for comparison with the previous year's activities

5. As a foreman, you observe that one of the men under your supervision seems to be rejected by the other men of the unit and tends to stay by himself.
Of the following, the MOST advisable course of action for you to take is to

    5.____

A. ignore the situation unless it interferes with the work of the unit
B. determine the reason and, if possible, attempt to rectify the situation
C. have the man transferred
D. inform the other men that they should change their attitude

6. The orders of a foreman are LEAST likely to be carried out properly if he   6._____

    A. gives detailed orders
    B. writes out his orders
    C. lacks patience when giving them
    D. asks for his orders to be repeated

Questions 7-8.

DIRECTIONS: Questions 7 and 8 are to be answered in accordance with the information
               given below.
    The specifications for a crankshaft main bearing journal are as follows:
        Diameter   - 2.2482" - 2.2490"
        Max. out-of-round -   .0004"
        Max. taper   -   .0003"/inch.
    A mechanic has measured a crankshaft main bearing journal on horizontal and vertical
axis, as shown in the diagram, and reported them as:

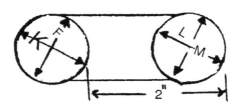

7. In accordance with the information given above, the measured journal   7._____

    A. is within specifications
    B. requires regrind due to excessive taper
    C. requires regrind due to excessive out-of-round
    D. requires regrind due to being undersize

8. In accordance with the information given above, if the mechanic reported measures of   8._____
                     F 2.2490"
                     K 2.2487"
                     L 2.2492"
                     M 2.2489"
the piece would be rejected as not meeting specifications because it is

    A. undersize   B. excessively out-of-round
    C. excessively tapered   D. oversize

9. The conditions of Emission Systems Warranties are usually based on regulations pro-   9._____
mulgated by the

    A. American Petroleum Institute
    B. Federal Clean Air Act

C. Environmental Protection Administration
D. Society of Automotive Engineers

10. After 6,000 miles of operation in approximately 6 months, it would be expected that motor vehicle warranties would cover

    A. ignition points with a loose pivot pin
    B. front wheel alignment
    C. a burned clutch disc
    D. a plugged fuel filter

10.____

11. In order to reduce harmful emissions, control of inlet air temperature to the carburetor is maintained by the _____ system.

    A. AIR   B. CCS
    C. PCV   D. Thermoactor

11.____

12. When you instruct one of your mechanics in the use of an ordinary oscilloscope for tuning an internal combustion engine, you should indicate to him that its use eliminates the need for a

    A. dwell meter   B. timing light
    C. compression tester   D. tachometer

12.____

Questions 13-16.

DIRECTIONS: Questions 13 through 16 are to be answered in accordance with the following information.
A *make* or *buy* decision must be made concerning pump shafts.
The shaft is 24 inches long and requires a cut-off, turning, and milling operation.
Material cost is $4.00/ft. Machining time and costs are as indicated:

	Initial Setup time (hrs.)	Mach. time/piece (hrs.)	Mach. rate/hr.
Cut-off	.5	.195	$ 5.00
Lathe	2.0	1.480	15.00
Mill	1.0	.500	10.00

13. With reference to the information given above, the minimum cost per piece based on producing these pump shafts in lots of 100 would be MOST NEARLY

    A. $17.40   B. $34.80   C. $36.60   D. $38.60

13.____

14. With reference to the information given above, the SMALLEST per unit cost for material and set-ups occurs in

    A. material   B. milling   C. turning   D. cut-off

14.____

15. With reference to the information given above, the GREATEST cost, per lot of 100 pieces, occurs in

    A. milling   B. material   C. turning   D. cut-off

15.____

16. With reference to the information given above, a steel supplier has quoted you a price of $750.00 for 100 pieces of stock to make the pump shafts. They would be delivered cut to length.
The amount saved per 100 shafts by purchasing from this supplier would be MOST NEARLY

    A. $50.00   B. $100.00   C. $150.00   D. $200.00

16._____

17. The State Department of Motor Vehicles excludes certain vehicles from the necessity of inspection.
Vehicles NOT excluded are

    A. front wheel drive passenger cars
    B. dump trucks equipped as snow plows
    C. police patrol cars
    D. road sweepers

17._____

18. The service brakes on a passenger car are to be inspected for issuance of a State Certificate of Inspection.
Of the following statements, the one that MOST correctly describes a procedure that must be followed or a condition that must exist before the certificate may be issued is

    A. one front and one rear brake drum must be removed
    B. the vehicle will be rejected if the pedal reserve is less than one-half of the total possible travel
    C. the master cylinder reservoir must be at least two-thirds full
    D. a brake equalization test must be performed

18._____

19. When a vehicle with a curved windshield is being inspected for issuance of a State Certificate of Inspection, it would be rejected if the windshield had

    A. cloudiness extending 11/2" from any edge
    B. four 3/4" diameter *stars* on any portion of the windshield
    C. a 9" crack and a 6" crack emanating from one point
    D. four 11/4" *stars,* one of which is located 2" from the bottom edge of the windshield

19._____

20. In connection with the boring of cylinders in an engine block, it is *desirable* that the crankshaft

    A. be in place and the main bearing caps be torqued to specifications
    B. be removed but the main bearing caps be replaced and torqued to specifications
    C. be in place and the main bearing caps be up hand tight
    D. and the main bearing caps be removed

20._____

21. Upon applying the brake after a failure in the primary (front brake) section of a dual master cylinder system, it would be noted that for the same stopping action as before the failure there would be

    A. increased pedal travel with increased pedal pressure
    B. increased pedal travel with no increase in pedal pressure
    C. no increase in pedal pressure or pedal travel
    D. increased pedal pressure with no increase in pedal travel

21._____

Questions 22-24.

DIRECTIONS: Questions 22 through 24, inclusive, are to be answered in accordance with the
following paragraph.

You have been instructed to expedite the fabrication of three special sand spreader
trucks using chassis that are available in the shop. All three trucks must be completed by
November 1. Based on workload and available hours, the foreman of the body shop indicates
that he could manufacture one complete sand spreader body per month, with one additional
week required for mounting and securing each body to the available chassis. No work could
begin on the body until the engines and hydraulic components, which would have to be purchased, were available for use. The Purchasing Department has promised the delivery of
engines and hydraulic components three months after the order is placed. (Assume that all
months have four weeks; and the same crew is doing the assembling and manufacturing.)

22.   With reference to the above paragraph, the LATEST date that the engines and associ-   22.____
ated hydraulic components could be requisitioned in order to meet the specified
deadline would be MOST NEARLY the end of the _____ week in _____.

A.   second; March   B.   first; April
C.   first; May   D.   first; June

23.   With reference to the above paragraph, the date of completion of the first sand spreader   23.____
truck, assuming that the Purchasing Department placed the order at the beginning
of the second week in February and ultimate delivery of the engines and components
was delayed by a month, would be MOST NEARLY the end of the _____ week in

_____.

A.   second; June   B.   fourth; June
C.   second; July   D.   fourth; July

24.   With reference to the above paragraph, the date of completion of the last sand spreader   24.____
truck, assuming that the Purchasing Department placed the order at the beginning of the
second week in February and actual delivery of the engines and components was made
two weeks early, would be MOST NEARLY the end of the _____ week in _____.

A.   second; August   B.   first; September
C.   third; September   D.   second; October

25.   A vacuum gage connected to the intake manifold of an idling V-8 gasoline engine reads   25.____
steady but low. The LEAST likely reason for this is

A.   late ignition timing
B.   late valve timing
C.   improper air-fuel mixture
D.   manifold air leaks

26.   The MOST likely cause of a metallic knock coming from the engine while running under   26.____
light load at 25 mph is

A.   a loose main bearing
B.   a loose piston pin
C.   a loose connecting rod bearing
D.   too early ignition timing

27. The usual procedure in making a battery capacity test is to draw a current   27.____

    A. equal to three times the ampere-hour rating for 15 seconds
    B. equal to the ampere-hour rating for 15 seconds
    C. equal to twice the ampere-hour rating for one minute
    D. adjusted to drop the battery voltage to two-thirds of its rated voltage in 15 seconds

28. A rectangularly shaped truck repair facility is 180 feet wide and 260 feet long. A 10-foot   28.____
space is provided along each wall for benches and equipment. A 60-foot wide area in the
middle of the floor is to remain clear for its entire 260-foot length. The entrance to the
shop is at one end of this open area.
Assuming that each truck occupies a working space 25 feet long and 12 feet wide, the
maximum number of trucks that could be parked perpendicularly to the 260-foot walls
(assuming no obstructions) would be MOST NEARLY

    A. 40   B. 60   C. 80   D. 120

29. If no spark is seen at the screwdriver tip when checking a distributor by shorting the mov-   29.____
able point to ground while the primary system is energized and the ignition points are
open, the MOST NEARLY correct statement that can be made is that

    A. this is normal in a properly operating ignition system
    B. the secondary circuit is open
    C. the condenser is shorted
    D. the points are defective

30. Ignition timing is MOST properly set   30.____

    A. with the vacuum advance line connected to the distributor
    B. prior to adjusting the point dwell
    C. with the engine running at a minimum speed of 1500 RPM
    D. after adjusting the point dwell

31. The vibration damper on an auto engine is fastened to the   31.____

    A. camshaft   B. flywheel
    C. crankshaft   D. driveshaft

32. Most small gas engines use a _____ ignition system.   32.____

    A. magneto   B. transistorized
    C. battery   D. induction

33. Carburetor icing occurs MOST often   33.____

    A. on humid, hot days
    B. when an engine is overheated
    C. on cool, damp days
    D. when an engine is run for long periods at idle speed

34. The function of the float in a carburetor is to   34.____

    A. close the needle valve
    B. control flow of gas into pump circuit
    C. operate choke circuit when engine is cold
    D. bleed off gasoline from primary tubes

35. To improve stability when cornering, manufacturers add a device to cars called a   35.____

    A. control arm   B. stabilizer bar
    C. constant velocity joint   D. Pitman arm

36. Adjustment of the tie rods on a car will affect   36.____

    A. camber   B. king pin inclination
    C. caster   D. toe-in

37. A restriction in the exhaust system is indicated on a vacuum gauge by a   37.____

    A. steady needle
    B. low reading
    C. gradual decrease in reading
    D. fast fluctuating needle

38. Disc brakes on a car have a distinct advantage over conventional drum brakes in that   38.____
they

    A. fade less when hot
    B. are cheaper to manufacture
    C. are easier to service
    D. require less pedal pressure to apply

39. In a diesel engine, the fuel is ignited by the   39.____

    A. spark plug   B. injector plug
    C. heat of compression   D. magneto

40. Engine timing is generally set by using a   40.____

    A. torque wrench   B. dividing head
    C. strobe light   D. centrifugal mechanism

41. If an engine is operated for long periods of time at part throttle opening, the   41.____

    A. spark plugs will become covered with carbon
    B. carburetor will become clogged
    C. fuel filter will accumulate more water
    D. points will blacken

42. Leaking intake valve guides will cause   42.____

    A. excessive oil consumption
    B. overheating
    C. valves to act sluggishly
    D. valve seats to burn

43. Flooding of a carburetor is generally caused by   43.____

    A. loose bolts holding carburetor to manifold
    B. air leaks in float bowl
    C. loose jets in carburetor body
    D. stuck float needle valve

44. On many cars, the fuel pump is combined with the   44.____

    A. vacuum pump   B. power steering pump
    C. generator   D. power brake booster

45. Carbon fouling of a spark plug is an indication of   45.____

    A. excessive oil burning   B. too rich a mixture
    C. poor grade of gasoline   D. plug misfiring

46. If tests show that generator output is excessive even after the *F* terminal has been dis-   46.____
connected, the trouble may be traced to

    A. the regulator   B. the generator
    C. poor ground   D. discharged battery

47. An automobile alternator converts alternating current to direct current by means of   47.____

    A. silicon diodes   B. a current regulator
    C. a solenoid coil   D. improper choke operation

48. Hard starting is very often caused by   48.____

    A. a faulty condenser   B. poor grade of gasoline
    C. improper grade of oil   D. improper choke operation

49. A car with a history of *burned points* would PROBABLY indicate   49.____

    A. improper gap setting
    B. improper condenser
    C. too high a setting of the voltage regulator
    D. incorrect dwell angle

50. When it is necessary to recondition brake drums, the MAXIMUM allowable amount of   50.____
oversize is _____".

    A. .025   B. .030   C. .040   D. .060

KEY (CORRECT ANSWERS)

1.	A	11.	B	21.	A	31.	C	41.	A
2.	A	12.	A	22.	B	32.	A	42.	A
3.	B	13.	C	23.	C	33.	C	43.	D
4.	B	14.	D	24.	A	34.	A	44.	A
5.	B	15.	C	25.	C	35.	B	45.	B
6.	C	16.	C	26.	C	36.	D	46.	B
7.	A	17.	A	27.	A	37.	C	47.	A
8.	D	18.	D	28.	C	38.	A	48.	D
9.	B	19.	D	29.	C	39.	C	49.	C
10.	A	20.	B	30.	D	40.	C	50.	D

TEST 2

DIRECTIONS: Each question or incomplete statement is followed by several suggested answers or completions. Select the one that BEST answers the question or completes the statement. *PRINT THE LETTER OF THE CORRECT ANSWER IN THE SPACE AT THE RIGHT.*

1. When starting a vehicle equipped with an alternator, the current from the battery generally flows to the alternator   1.____

   A. commutator   B. stator windings
   C. rotor windings   D. rectifier

2. Assume that in a repair job it becomes necessary to expand the piston skirt so that the   2.____
   piston-to-cylinder clearance becomes one-half of that normally required.
   Of the following methods of expanding piston skirts, the one which is BEST used to obtain the above results is

   A. pressure and heat   B. knurling
   C. peening   D. spring expanders

3. The statement that is MOST NEARLY correct concerning vapor lock in an operating   3.____
   engine is that

   A. the more volatile the fuel the greater the tendency for it to vapor lock
   B. the tendency to vapor lock is decreased by hard driving
   C. the tendency to vapor lock is decreased when driving at high altitude
   D. minor defects in engine cooling contributes greatly to vapor lock

4. Of the following statements concerning cylindrical and centerless grinders, the one which   4.____
   is MOST NEARLY correct is:

   A. The *through-feed* method of work handling is applicable to the cylindrical grinder
   B. Less metal needs to be removed to produce a round piece of work on a centerless grinder
   C. Internal grinding of cylindrical objects cannot be done on a centerless grinder
   D. To grind a piece of work of different diameters in a centerless grinder, the work piece must be fed on one side and ejected on the other side

5. Many cars are equipped with a device that varies the spark angle with manifold vacuum.   5.____
   When the manifold vacuum suddenly increases, it is likely that the angle of spark

   A. advances
   B. remains the same as before
   C. decreases
   D. is retarded

6. Assume that engine tightening specifications for the cylinder head bolts on a late model   6.____
   Chevrolet is 95 ft.lbs. If the wrench available has an effective leverage of 15", the force necessary to satisfactorily tighten the bolts
   is MOST NEARLY _____ lbs.

   A. 6.3   B. 47.0   C. 75.0   D. 118.8

7. In connection with power brakes on an operating vehicle, the statement MOST NEARLY   7.____
correct is:

   A. Air-suspended units are under vacuum pressure until the brakes are applied
   B. Vacuum-suspended units are balanced with atmospheric pressure until the brakes
      are applied
   C. Vacuum-suspended units are unbalanced by means of the engine vacuum when
      the pedal is depressed
   D. Air-suspended units are unbalanced by means of the engine vacuum when the
      pedal is depressed

8. In reboring a diesel cylinder block bore to receive a new 4.631"-.001" O.D. liner, the MAX-   8.____
IMUM allowable block bore should generally be

   A. 4.626"   B. 4.627"   C. 4.632"   D. 4.634"

9. A common rail system of fuel injection is BEST described as a system using a   9.____

   A. single pump for compressing the fuel, plus a metering element for each cylinder
   B. single pump for metering and compressing the fuel, plus a dividing device for sup-
      plying the fuel to the various cylinders
   C. separate metering and compressing pump for each cylinder of the engine
   D. single pump for compressing the fuel, plus a transfer pump to meter the fuel for
      each cylinder

10. Assume that a storage floor area of 300 square feet can safely support 120 lbs. per sq.ft.   10.____
The MAXIMUM number of 50-gallon oil drums that can be stored on this floor is MOST
NEARLY (assume one gallon of water weighs 8.3 lbs. and the specific gravity of oil is
.85)

   A. 210   B. 105   C. 87   D. 75

11. A Brinell number of 450 corresponds MOST NEARLY to a Rockwell C number of   11.____

   A. 52   B. 48   C. 40   D. 35

12. The one of the following which causes the front wheels of a car to right themselves after   12.____
a turn is the

   A. toe-in   B. camber
   C. side thrust   D. caster

13. The process used to produce only a superficially hard wear-resisting surface on a   13.____
machined part is generally called

   A. nitriding   B. tempering
   C. flame hardening   D. cyaniding

14. When a gasoline engine is idling with no external load, it usually demands a rich mixture   14.____
or charge.
The MOST probable reason for this is that

   A. when the intake valve opens, a higher pressure exists in the cylinder than in the
      intake manifold
   B. when the throttle is near the closed position, the pressure at the end of the exhaust
      stroke is always below atmospheric

    C.   when the throttle is near the closed position, the pressure in the intake manifold is above atmospheric

    D.   inert exhaust gas increases the explosive mixture or charge

15. Cam ground pistons are used PRIMARILY because   15._____

    A.   they can be used in badly worn engines without reboring the cylinders
    B.   their use increases the compression ratio
    C.   their use aids in the lubrication of the cylinder walls
    D.   they eliminate piston slap in engine warm-up and permit expansion

16. After a D.C. generator has been repaired and installed in a passenger car, it must be   16._____
polarized.
If the generator field is externally grounded, the BEST procedure to follow in polarizing the generator is to

    A.   just touch with a jumper between terminals marked *Gen* and *Bat* of the voltage regulator
    B.   disconnect the field wire from the regulator and touch this wire to the regulator *Bat* terminal
    C.   disconnect the field wire from the regulator and touch this wire to the *Gen* terminal
    D.   just touch with a jumper between terminals marked *Gen* and *Field* of the voltage regulator

17. The outside surfaces of aluminum alloy pistons are usually made highly resistant to wear   17._____
by means of which one of the following methods?

    A.   Induction hardening   B.   Anodizing
    C.   Normalizing   D.   Spheroidizing

18. The temperature of the burning air-fuel mixture in an internal combustion gasoline   18._____
engine is MOST NEARLY _____°F.

    A.   1000   B.   1500   C.   2500   D.   4500

19. Assume that after removing the cylinder head of an engine, a wet, oily condition is   19._____
noticed on the block between two adjacent cylinders.
This is PROBABLY caused by

    A.   a ruptured pump diaphragm
    B.   a scored cylinder wall
    C.   worn valve guides
    D.   a blown cylinder head gasket

20. Assume that the valve timing diagram of a Cadillac engine shows the intake valve   20._____
opened for a period of 290°.

The distance that this 290° represents on the circumference of an 18" flywheel is
MOST NEARLY

    A.   28.5"   B.   37.5"   C.   45.5"   D.   52.5"

21. Assume that a job order calls for an AISI-3115 or a S.A.E.-3120 steel to be used in the   21.____
fabrication of an automotive component.
This material is MOST likely a _____ steel.

   A. silicon-manganese   B. nickel-chromium
   C. chromium   D. manganese

22. A pinging sound in an engine is most likely to occur on open throttle at low or moderate   22.____
engine speed.
This pinging is further increased by which one of the following conditions?

   A. Use of high octane fuel
   B. Heavy carbon deposits in cylinder
   C. Low atmospheric temperature
   D. Intake manifold heater valve in the *off* position when engine is warm

23. A key factor in lathe development today has been the introduction of new cutting tool   23.____
materials. Of the following, the LATEST material in lathe cutting tools is

   A. stellite   B. cemented-carbide
   C. cast alloys   D. ceramics

24. A regulator used to control the output of an alternator usually consists of a number of   24.____
parts.
The one of the following which is NOT a part of this type of regulator is the

   A. load relay   B. current limiter
   C. voltage regulator   D. reverse-current relay

25. Shoulder wear on both sides of treads of a rubber tire is PROBABLY caused by   25.____

   A. overinflation
   B. cornering
   C. underinflation
   D. incorrect toe-in or toe-out

26. Of the following types of alloy bearings, the one that requires a bearing wall of substantial   26.____
thickness if it is NOT bonded to a steel back is

   A. aluminum   B. copper
   C. cadmium   D. tin-base babbit

27. When a particular piston of a gasoline engine is in a *rock* position, it may CORRECTLY   27.____
be said that the

   A. crankshaft can move about $25°$ without causing the valves to open or close
   B. piston has reached the bottom of its stroke
   C. crankshaft cannot move without causing the piston to move
   D. crankshaft can move a bout $15°$ without causing the piston to move up or down

28. A grinding wheel marked C14-N12-S20 would be used MOST effectively for grinding   28.____

   A. cast iron   B. a milling cutter
   C. SAE 1330 steel   D. SAE 1090 steel

29. To test for leaks around the intake manifold of an idling engine, the mechanic would   29.____
    MOST likely use

    A. soap bubbles   B. talc powder
    C. oil   D. heavy grease

30. When assembling a gear-type oil pump, used on passenger cars, the end clearance on   30.____
    the inside of the pump must be MOST NEARLY

    A. .001"   B. .003"   C. .006"   D. .010"

31. Of the following descriptions of engine noises, the one that is USUALLY associated with   31.____
    the valve mechanism is a

    A. light rap or clattering with a light load at approximately 25 MPH
    B. click, snap or sharp rattle on acceleration
    C. sharp, metallic, double-knock with the engine idling
    D. clicking sound occurring at regular intervals

32. Assume when using a vacuum gauge to troubleshoot an engine which does not have   32.____
    overlapping valve timing,
    it is noticed that the needle on the vacuum gauge drifts slowly back and forth. This
    generally indicates

    A. poor air-fuel mixture
    B. an air leak in the intake manifold
    C. late valve timing
    D. a blown cylinder head gasket

33. Assume that a rectangular concrete shop floor, 100 feet x 125 feet, is to be painted with   33.____
    two coats of paint.
    If the paint covers 450 square feet per gallon on the first coat and 900 square feet per
    gallon on the second coat, the total number of gallons of paint required to do the above
    job is MOST NEARLY

    A. 30   B. 36   C. 42   D. 48

34. Assume a 1/2" hole is drilled 1 1/2" off-center on a 4" diameter circular disc.   34.____
    If a shaft is keyed through the 1/2" hole and the disc is used as a cam, the lift of the
    cam will be

    A. 2 3/4"   B. 3"   C. 3 1/4"   D. 3 1/2"

35. In a diesel engine, good combustion is BEST obtained when the diesel fuel is burned in   35.____
    the presence of MOST NEARLY _____ excess air.

    A. no   B. 10%
    C. 60 to 70%   D. 100 to 150%

36. For most passenger cars used by the various departments, the crankshaft end play in a   36.____
    reassembled engine should be HOST NEARLY

    A. .001"   B. .005"   C. .010"   D. .015"

37. Assume that a Ford Transistorized Ignition System uses a 2 mfd condenser in the ampli- 37.____
fier assembly.
The function of this condenser is to

    A. discharge its current directly into the secondary high voltage circuit
    B. prevent metal build-up on the distributor points similar to the conventional ignition
       system
    C. absorb high inductive energy during initial distributor point opening
    D. discharge energy into the primary coil at the same moment as the battery current s
       the primary coil

38. Assume that a 12 spline shape is to be cut on a shaft in a milling machine. 38.____
If the shaft diameter is 1 5/8", the index plate circle to use is MOST NEARLY

    A. 20   B. 19   C. 17   D. 15

39. A light spring expander is used in conjunction with piston rings to increase the wall pres- 39.____
sure in slightly worn or tapered cylinders.
This expander is USUALLY located _____ ring.

    A. below the scraper   B. above the compression
    C. behind the scraper   D. behind the compression

40. Assume that the breakdown cost of a particular motor job is as follows: 40.____

        Parts $160.00
        Labor   75.00
        Overhead   30.00

The percentage of the total cost for labor is MOST NEARLY

    A. 20%   B. 25%   C. 28%   D. 32%

41. Setting the spark plug gap opening closer than normally required would PROBABLY 41.____
result in _____ idling and _____ in top engine speed.

    A. smoother; increase   B. rougher; decrease
    C. smoother; decrease   D. rougher; increase

42. If air should be trapped within the fuel pump of a solid injection diesel engine, it is likely 42.____
that

    A. no fuel would be delivered
    B. the pump discharge pressure will increase
    C. the charge of the fuel to the engine will be lean
    D. a mixture of fuel and air would be delivered

43.   43.____

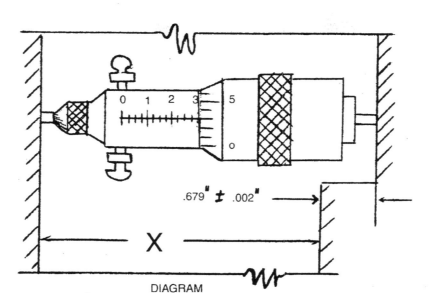

DIAGRAM

With the thimble at the zero setting, the overall length (of the above diagram) of the inside type micrometer measures exactly 2.500".
When the micrometer is opened as shown above, the MINIMUM distance for X is MOST NEARLY

A.   1.819"   B.   1.852"   C.   2.122"   D.   2.149"

44. During a three-minute battery test of a 12V battery, if the cell voltages are uneven by   44.____
more than 0.1V or 0.15V, the mechanic should

A.   test total battery voltage with charger still operating on fast charge
B.   test electrolyte specific gravity and charge battery
C.   replace the battery
D.   add electrolyte, charge the battery slowly, and re-test

45. The piston ring end clearance of a ring installed in the top groove of a piston for a 31/4"   45.____
cylinder bore is MOST NEARLY

A.   0.004"   B.   0.007"   C.   0.009"   D.   0.013"

46. The gas pressure in the hose of the acetylene line supplying an ordinary oxy-acetylene   46.____
welding torch, when the torch is in operation, should be kept between _____ psi.

A.   1-15   B.   30-45   C.   50-75   D.   75-100

47. Water sludge in engine crankcase oil is MOST usually caused by   47.____

A.   using a low viscosity oil
B.   condensation in the crankcase
C.   mixing different brands of motor oil
D.   using a high viscosity oil

48. In a typical Chrysler Torque Flite three-speed transmission, the band-clutch applications for drive position -2nd speed are
    48._____

    A. front and rear clutches
    B. front clutch and kickdown band
    C. front clutch and overrunning clutch
    D. kickdown and overrunning clutch

49. Of the following parts of a crankcase ventilation system, the one that is NOT a part of the positive-type crankcase ventilating system is the
    49._____

    A. intake breather
    B. road draft tube
    C. manifold suction tube
    D. metering valve

50. A *cylinder balance test* is NOT usually used to locate
    50._____

    A. worn piston rings
    B. a leaky intake manifold
    C. a defective spark plug
    D. a valve not opening properly due to a worm cam shaft

KEY (CORRECT ANSWERS)

1.	C	11.	B	21.	B	31.	D	41.	D
2.	B	12.	A	22.	B	32.	A	42.	A
3.	A	13.	D	23.	D	33.	C	43.	C
4.	B	14.	A	24.	D	34.	B	44.	C
5.	A	15.	D	25.	C	35.	C	45.	D
6.	C	16.	A	26.	A	36.	B	46.	A
7.	D	17.	B	27.	C	37.	C	47.	B
8.	C	18.	D	28.	A	38.	D	48.	B
9.	A	19.	D	29.	C	39.	C	49.	B
10.	B	20.	C	30.	B	40.	C	50.	A

EXAMINATION SECTION
TEST 1

DIRECTIONS: Each question or incomplete statement is followed by several suggested answers or completions. Select the one that BEST answers the question or completes the statement. *PRINT THE LETTER OF THE CORRECT ANSWER IN THE SPACE AT THE RIGHT.*

1. The gage that is generally used in the United States for sizing non-ferrous wires and non-ferrous sheets is the

    A. Birmingham Wire Gage
    B. Brown & Sharpe Wire Gage
    C. United States Standard (Revised)
    D. Stubs Wire Gage

1.____

2. The number of threads per inch for a screw with a pitch of .3125" is MOST NEARLY

    A. 3 1/4   B. 4 1/4   C. 2 1/4   D. 5 1/4

2.____

3. A center gage is used to check

    A. cylinder bore diameters   B. tapers
    C. 60° threading tools   D. lines on rough work

3.____

4. The portion of a gear tooth between the pitch circle and the root circle is called the

    A. clearance   B. dedendum
    C. addendum   D. pressure angle

4.____

5. Which one of the following is NOT used as an abrasive for lapping?

    A. Emery   B. Alundum
    C. Diamond dust   D. Quartz

5.____

6. If the air gap between the pole pieces and armature of a generator increases due to worn bearings, the result would be

    A. a decrease in generator output
    B. an increase in magnetic lines of force
    C. an increase in generator output
    D. no change in the number of magnetic lines of force

6.____

7. When the generator is not operating on a passenger car, the cutout relay USUALLY

    A. closes the circuit between the generator and battery
    B. sends residual current through the circuit to supply the electrical equipment
    C. prevents any damaging current to flow from the battery to the electrical devices
    D. prevents the battery from discharging back through the generator

7.____

8. In looking over an alteration job on car bodies, you find that 96 pieces of 1" x 1" x 1'6" long square steel stock are needed to do this job. Steel weighs 480 lbs. per cu.ft. and costs $0.12 per lb.
The total cost of this material is MOST NEARLY

    A. $40.00   B. $60.00   C. $80.00   D. $100.00

8.____

9. The Shore's Scleroscope is an instrument which measures the hardness of materials by means of a 9.____

    A. steel ball
    B. diamond penetrator
    C. diamond-tipped hammer
    D. square-based diamond pyramid

10. A process of annealing white cast iron in which the carbon is wholly or in part transformed to graphitic or free carbon, and, in some cases, part of the carbon is removed completely, is called 10.____

    A. spheroidizing
    B. carburizing
    C. malleablizing
    D. nitriding

11. Relative to driving axles, which one of the following statements is MOST NEARLY correct? 11.____

    A. The types of live axles are distinguished by the way in which the axle shafts are connected and the stresses they must carry.
    B. For plain live axles, all stresses caused by turning corners, skidding, or wobbling wheels are not taken by the axle shafts.
    C. In the semifloating axle, the differential case is carried on the inner ends of the axle shafts.
    D. In a fullfloating rear axle, the axle shafts are rigidly connected to the wheels.

12. A passenger car is equipped with a fluid coupling and an automatic transmission. When the engine is idling and the vehicle is stationary, the percentage *slip* is MOST NEARLY 12.____

    A. 100   B. 80   C. 10   D. 2

13. In front wheel alignment work, the term *axle caster* is defined as the 13.____

    A. amount the wheels incline at the top from a vertical position
    B. outward inclination of wheels at top
    C. backward inclination between the steering knuckle kingpin and the vertical plane
    D. run out of the front wheels with respect to the steering knuckle kingpin

14. Which one of the following statements concerning milling machine operations is MOST NEARLY true? 14.____

    A. Climb-milling means that the feeding movement of the work and the cutting movement are in opposite directions.
    B. Conventional-milling means that the feeding movement of the work and the cutting movement are in the same direction.
    C. Cutters used in the conventional-milling manner tend to seat the work firmly in the holding device.
    D. The cutters used in climb-milling tend to seat the work firmly in the holding devices.

15. Crankshafts are USUALLY manufactured of 15.____

    A. steel and nickel
    B. iron and vanadium
    C. steel and cobalt
    D. steel and tungsten

16. In brazing, the filler metal GENERALLY   16._____

    A. is a ferrous metal or alloy
    B. is heated only to a red heat
    C. has a melting point lower than 1000° F
    D. has a melting point lower than that of the base metals to be joined

17. In welding certain alloy steels with electric arc welding, the effect of a coating on the elec-   17._____
trode is to

    A. reduce arc stability
    B. increase attractive force between molten metal and the end of the electrode
    C. protect the molten weld metal from the ambient atmosphere while cooling
    D. provide ingredients which, when melted, prevent formation of slag over molten
       metal

18. In the operation of a 6-cylinder, 4-cycle diesel engine, you observe that the engine is   18._____
missing erratically or intermittently on all cylinders.
The trouble in this case is MOST likely NOT due to

    A. sticking nozzle valve
    B. plugged air cleaner
    C. improper fuel
    D. badly worn piston pins or bushings

19. In a *common rail* system of fuel injection as used in many high-speed diesel engines, the   19._____
pressure, in lbs. per sq. in., maintained by the master pump is MOST NEARLY

    A. 6,000   B. 15,000   C. 500   D. 150

20. The SMALLEST diameter of a circular steel plate from which a 7/8" square can be cut is   20._____
MOST NEARLY

    A. 0.951"   B. 1.279"   C. 1.217"   D. 1.237"

21. A large majority of industrial applications require that motor speeds remain approxi-   21._____
mately constant under all conditions of loading. Lathes and milling machines are examples.
The D.C. motor which meets the above conditions is MOST NEARLY a _____ motor.

    A. series   B. shunt
    C. induction   D. wound-rotor

22. In timing the fuel injection of a 4-cycle diesel engine, when the end of compression is   22._____
reached,

    A. both intake and exhaust valves are open
    B. the intake valve only is closed
    C. the exhaust valve only is closed
    D. both intake and exhaust valves are closed

23. The ease with which gasoline and other liquids vaporize or pass from the liquid to a   23._____
vapor state is known as its

    A. kinematic viscosity   B. viscous friction
    C. volatility   D. surface viscosity

24. Suppose a piece of work on a milling machine requires 69 divisions, and this is to be done by means of compound indexing.
Which one of the following indexing movements would you suggest your machinist to use to do this job?

    A. 9/21 + 3/33
    B. 21/23 - 11/33
    C. 23/29 - 11/33
    D. 3/31 + 11/33

24._____

25. A gear with 80 teeth is driven by a pinion having 30 teeth.
If the pinion gear revolves at 600 RPM, the speed of the gear, in revolutions per minute, is MOST NEARLY

    A. 225   B. 1600   C. 200   D. 1500

25._____

26. In cam grinding pistons, you observe that the grinding wheel becomes glazed frequently.
In order to remedy this condition, you should substitute another wheel which has a

    A. harder bond
    B. softer bond
    C. larger diameter
    D. smaller diameter

26._____

27. A replacement part for a truck engine is to be made from S.A.E. 4140 steel.
This type of steel is MOST likely a _____ steel.

    A. molybdenum
    B. nickel
    C. chrome-nickel
    D. chrome vanadium

27._____

28. The mechanical efficiency of a gasoline engine is obtained by dividing the brake horse-power by the

    A. S.A.E. horsepower
    B. indicated horsepower
    C. volumetric horsepower
    D. thermal efficiency

28._____

29. An empty truck weighs 4,000 lbs., and its center of gravity is 100 inches in front of the rear axle. The truck carries a load of 3,000 lbs., and the center of gravity of this load is 50 inches in front of the rear axle.
If the wheel base is 150 inches, then the total weight on the rear wheels is MOST NEARLY _____ lbs.

    A. 3525   B. 3625   C. 3425   D. 3325

29._____

30. A hydraulic hoisting cylinder on a truck operates with a pressure of 800 lbs. per sq.in. The piston has a diameter of 3.25 inches.
The maximum load, in tons, that can be raised is MOST NEARLY

    A. 5   B. 4   C. 3   D. 6

30._____

31. Relative to an Auto-Lite vacuum advance mechanism of the type which is mounted on the side of the distributor, the basic principle of operation is that the

    A. spring retards the spark and the vacuum advances it
    B. spring retards and advances the spark
    C. vacuum retards the spark and the spring advances it
    D. vacuum retards and advances the spark

31._____

32. The condenser that is used in the distributor circuit of an auto ignition system is   32.____

    A. usually an electrolytic type condenser
    B. below the required capacity if the breaker lever contact develops a pitted cavity
    C. under normal operating conditions, usually about .250 microfarads
    D. usually about 0.5 microfarad

33. During discharge, the internal resistance of a storage battery   33.____

    A. decreases   B. remains the same
    C. is negative   D. increases

34. In low speed, a passenger car has a 2.39 to 1 transmission ratio.   34.____
If, at the rear, the drive pinion has 10 teeth and the bevel gear has 39 teeth, then the
total reduction ratio (engine shaft to rear wheels) for this low speed is MOST NEARLY

    A. 3.39   B. 3.90   C. 6.39   D. 9.32

35. In an air brake system, the relay valve is USUALLY installed between the   35.____

    A. brake chambers and the compressor
    B. compressor and the reservoir
    C. brake valve and the quick release valve
    D. reservoir and the brake chambers

36. With reference to a vibrating relay voltage regulator, which one of the following state-   36.____
ments is TRUE?

    A. With this regulator, the voltage output of the generator is not used for automatic
        regulation.
    B. The voltage coil is connected across the generator brushes and is wound with
        heavy wire.
    C. The voltage coil is usually connected in series with the storage battery.
    D. If a break occurs in the voltage regulator circuit at high speeds, an excessive
        charging rate will result.

37. The object of a vibration damper on the crankshaft of multi-cylinder engines is to   37.____

    A. act as a counterweight for the flywheel and absorb the end thrust
    B. maintain the leverage of the crankshaft with respect to the flywheel
    C. resist the sudden movements of the cranks due to torsional twisting of the crank-
        shaft
    D. offset the centrifugal force developed by the rotating crankpins and connecting
        rods

38. Which one of the following statements concerning hydramatic transmissions is MOST   38.____
NEARLY CORRECT?

    A. When the clutch is released and the band applied on the front planetary unit, the
        unit is in reduction.
    B. When the band is released and the clutch applied on the front planetary, the unit is
        in reduction.
    C. The front planetary unit is for direct drive and the rear planetary unit is for reduc-
        tion.
    D. The front servo is applied by spring pressure and released by oil pressure.

39. The primary circuit of a typical electric ignition system consists basically of   39.____

    A. condenser, primary element of the distributor, primary winding of the coil, and low voltage current source
    B. low voltage current source, secondary winding of the coil, condenser, and primary element of the distributor
    C. primary element of the distributor, condenser, spark plug, and low voltage current source
    D. low voltage current source, primary winding of the coil, secondary winding of the coil, and condenser

40. Which one of the following statements is MOST NEARLY CORRECT?   40.____

    A. A jack may be used for a load in excess of its rated capacity.
    B. When preparing electrolyte, the water should be poured into the acid.
    C. Gasoline containing tetraethyl lead may be used to clean automobile parts.
    D. For combating electrical fires, CO_2 type extinguishers should be used.

KEY (CORRECT ANSWERS)

1. B	11. A	21. B	31. A
2. A	12. A	22. D	32. C
3. C	13. C	23. C	33. D
4. B	14. D	24. B	34. D
5. D	15. A	25. A	35. D
6. A	16. D	26. B	36. D
7. D	17. C	27. A	37. C
8. B	18. D	28. B	38. A
9. C	19. A	29. D	39. A
10. C	20. D	30. C	40. D

EXAMINATION SECTION
TEST 1

DIRECTIONS: Each question or incomplete statement is followed by several suggested answers or completions. Select the one that BEST answers the question or completes the statement. *PRINT THE LETTER OF THE CORRECT ANSWER IN THE SPACE AT THE RIGHT.*

1. Of the following, the one that is a grease fitting is a _____ fitting. 1.____

   A. Morse
   C. Zerk
   B. Brown and Sharpe
   D. Caliper

2. In an automobile equipped with an ammeter, the ammeter is used to 2.____

   A. indicate current flow
   B. regulate current flow
   C. act as a circuit breaker
   D. measure engine r.p.m.

3. The ignition points in the distributor of a gasoline engine are opened by means of a 3.____

   A. spring
   C. cam with lobes
   B. vacuum
   D. gear

4. MOST automobile engines that use gasoline as fuel operate as _____ cycle engines. 4.____

   A. single
   C. two-stroke, two-
   B. single stroke, single
   D. four-stroke, two-

5. When making a hole in a concrete floor for a machine hold-down bolt, the BEST tool to use is a 5.____

   A. star drill
   C. cold chisel
   B. drift punch
   D. counterboring tool

6. When cutting a hole through a 1/2-inch thick wooden partition, the BEST type of saw to use from among the following choices is a _____ saw. 6.____

   A. coping   B. back   C. rip   D. saber

7. An anodized finish is USUALLY associated with 7.____

   A. aluminum
   C. cast iron
   B. steel
   D. brass

8. Certain devices are used to transmit power from one shaft to another. A device that does so WITHOUT the use of friction is a 8.____

   A. square jaw clutch
   C. compression coupling
   B. simple disk clutch
   D. thermocouple

9. If it is necessary to check the true temperature setting of a thermostat for a shop unit heater, it would be BEST to use 9.____

   A. a mercury thermometer near the heater
   B. a mercury thermometer near the thermostat

C. another similar thermostat near the thermostat to be tested
D. a standard thermostat

10. To remove a shrink-fitted collar from a shaft, it would be EASIEST to drive out the shaft   10.____
after

    A. *chilling* the collar and heating the shaft
    B. *chilling* only the collar
    C. *heating* only the collar
    D. *heating* both the collar and the shaft

11. When drilling a hole in a broken machine stud in order to remove the stud with an extrac-   11.____
tor, it is BEST to drill the hole

    A. off-center
    B. in the center
    C. with the smallest diameter drill possible
    D. with a taper

12. When fitting two steel parts together, steel dowel pins are GENERALLY used to   12.____

    A. keep the parts securely fastened together
    B. provide a wide tolerance fit
    C. provide an adjustable clearance space between the two parts
    D. secure exact placement of these parts with respect to each other

13. When storing files, it is important that they do not touch each other.   13.____
The PRIMARY reason for this is to prevent

    A. damage to the handles
    B. dirt from collecting in the teeth
    C. damage to the teeth
    D. rusting

14. The frequency of lubrication of bearings and other moving parts of machinery depends   14.____
PRIMARILY on

    A. the amount of their use   B. their size
    C. the direction of motion   D. the operator's judgment

15. To determine whether the surface of a work bench is horizontal, the BEST tool to use is a   15.____

    A. surface gage   B. plumb bob
    C. feeler gage   D. spirit level

16. The swing on a lathe refers to the   16.____

    A. distance between centers of the head and tail spindles
    B. size of the face plate
    C. speed range of the gears in r.p.m.
    D. diameter of the largest workpiece that can be turned

17. When installing new piston rings in an air compressor, the piston ring gap is BEST mea-   17.____
    sured by using a(n)

    A. outside caliper   B. feeler gage
    C. depth gage   D. inside caliper

18. When cutting external threads on a pipe, the tool that ACTUALLY cuts the thread is   18.____
    called a

    A. tap   B. die   C. reamer   D. hone

19. A dynamometer would be MOST useful in   19.____

    A. measuring angles on a steel plate
    B. determining the operating efficiency of an engine
    C. pumping hot fluids out of a tank
    D. heating large shop areas

20. A screw-thread micrometer is used PRIMARILY to measure   20.____

    A. pitch diameter   B. thread height
    C. major diameter   D. thread lead

21. A compound-pressure gage found on certain types of equipment is used to indicate   21.____

    A. the sum of two pressures
    B. the difference between two pressures
    C. either vacuum or pressure
    D. two different pressures simultaneously

22. Of the following, the machine screw having the SMALLEST diameter is   22.____

    A. 6-32 x 11/2"   B. 8-32 x 3/4"
    C. 10-24 x 1"   D. 12-24 x1/2"

23. A good quality precision compression spring would MOST probably have   23.____

    A. a small diameter and small wire size
    B. its ends ground flat
    C. a large diameter and large wire size
    D. a high spring rate

24. From among the following materials, the MOST fireproof one for use in maintenance   24.____
    work is

    A. canvas   B. nylon   C. cotton   D. asbestos

25. The metal which has the GREATEST tendency to crack when dropped onto a hard sur-   25.____
    face is

    A. rolled steel   B. forged steel
    C. wrought iron   D. cast iron

26. When using a portable electric drill having a 3-conductor cord, it is IMPORTANT from a   26.____
    safety point of view that

    A. the drill is run at fairly slow speeds
    B. high-speed drill bits should be used

C. the power outlet has a ground connection
D. the drill is run on 3-phase current

27. The MOST efficient way of laying out a 25-foot long, straight line on a concrete floor is to   27.____

    A. use a carpenter's pencil and a steel tape
    B. lay out a cord and mark the line with a crayon
    C. use chalk and a 6-foot ruler
    D. snap it on with a chalked mason's line

28. The MAIN advantage of using pipes instead of timber for temporary scaffolding is that   28.____
    pipe scaffolding

    A. requires no painting
    B. is easier to assemble and disassemble
    C. requires no bracing
    D. looks better

29. In order to avoid damage to an air compressor, the air coming into it is USUALLY   29.____

    A. cooled   B. metered   C. filtered   D. heated

30. If a gear having 24 teeth is revolving at 150 r.p.m., then the speed of an 8-tooth pinion   30.____
    driving the gear is _____ r.p.m.

    A. 50   B. 300   C. 450   D. 1200

31. To preserve wood from rotting, it is BEST to use   31.____

    A. aluminum paint   B. red lead
    C. rosin   D. creosote

32. On a two-stage air compressor, the intercooler is connected to the compressor unit   32.____

    A. *between* the two stages
    B. *after* the second stage
    C. *before* the first stage
    D. *between* the receiver and the outlet

33. Teflon is COMMONLY used as a(n)   33.____

    A. protective coating on ceramic plumbing fixtures
    B. sealer on threaded pipe joints
    C. additive to engine lubricating oil
    D. penetrating oil for rusting parts

34. A marline spike is GENERALLY used to   34.____

    A. splice manila rope
    B. fasten a heavy metal part to a wood panel wall
    C. shift large crates
    D. anchor wooden items to a concrete wall

35. A screw having double threads is one that   35.____

    A. should never be used for fastening sheet metal parts
    B. has two parallel threads running in the same direction
    C. has a right hand and a left hand thread
    D. can be used with a mating single-threaded nut

36. If the diameter of a circular piece of sheet metal is 11/2 feet, the area, in square inches,   36.____
is MOST NEARLY

    A. 1.77   B. 2.36   C. 254   D. 324

37. When removing a cartridge-type fuse from the fuse clips in a circuit, it is important to use   37.____
a fuse-puller PRIMARILY to avoid

    A. blowing the fuse   B. damaging the fuse
    C. arcing   D. personal injury

38. The MOST probable cause for the breaking of a drill bit while drilling into a steel plate is   38.____

    A. excessive drill pressure
    B. a hard spot in the steel
    C. a drill speed which is too low
    D. too much cutting-oil lubricant

39. In assembling structural steel, a drift pin is used to   39.____

    A. line up holes
    B. punch holes
    C. temporarily hold welded parts
    D. knock out structural bolts

40. The TIGHTEST fit for a mating shaft and hole is a _____ fit.   40.____

    A. running   B. sliding   C. working   D. force

KEY (CORRECT ANSWERS)

1.	C	11.	B	21.	C	31.	D
2.	A	12.	D	22.	A	32.	A
3.	C	13.	C	23.	B	33.	B
4.	D	14.	A	24.	D	34.	A
5.	A	15.	D	25.	D	35.	B
6.	D	16.	D	26.	C	36.	C
7.	A	17.	B	27.	D	37.	D
8.	A	18.	B	28.	B	38.	A
9.	B	19.	B	29.	C	39.	A
10.	C	20.	A	30.	C	40.	D

TEST 2

DIRECTIONS: Each question or incomplete statement is followed by several suggested answers or completions. Select the one that BEST answers the question or completes the statement. *PRINT THE LETTER OF THE CORRECT ANSWER IN THE SPACE AT THE RIGHT.*

1. The crankshaft in a gasoline engine is PRIMARILY used to

   A. change reciprocating motion to rotary motion
   B. operate the valve lifters
   C. supply power to each cylinder
   D. function as a flywheel

1.____

2. Copper tubing is GENERALLY used in an annealed condition because annealing

   A. gives the copper tubing a protective finish
   B. makes the copper tubing harder
   C. provides a smoother surface on the inner and outer walls
   D. makes the copper tubing more ductile

2.____

3. Of the following, the MOST important advantage of a ratchet wrench as compared to an open-end wrench is that the ratchet wrench

   A. is adjustable
   B. cannot strip the threads of a nut
   C. can be used in a limited space
   D. measures the force applied

3.____

4. To provide a close-fitting hole for a taper pin, it is BEST to first drill the hole and then to use the appropriate

   A. hone   B. reamer
   C. boring tool   D. counterboring tool

4.____

5. If a part that is being checked for size fits loosely into a *NO-GO* gauge, it means that the

   A. part is the proper size
   B. part must be made smaller
   C. part is the wrong size
   D. gauge should be tightened

5.____

6. A hacksaw blade with 32 teeth per inch is BEST for cutting

   A. materials less than 1/8-inch thick
   B. a 3-inch diameter brass bar
   C. 1" thick copper plates
   D. a 3-inch diameter steel bar

6.____

7. The BEST method to follow in order to prevent a drill from wandering upon starting to drill a hole in a steel plate is to

   A. use a high-speed drill
   B. first use a center-punch

7.____

C. use a drill with even cutting angles
D. exert heavy pressure when drilling

8. When grinding a tool, it is GOOD practice to keep moving the tool across the face of the grinding wheel in order to

    8.____

    A. prevent the tool from becoming too hot
    B. avoid sparks
    C. maintain a uniform grinding speed
    D. prevent grooving the wheel

9. A material that is COMMONLY used as a lining for bearings in order to reduce friction is

    9.____

    A. magnesium   B. cast iron
    C. babbitt   D. carborundum

10. In a motor having sleeve bearings, bearing wear can be checked by measuring the air-gap clearance between the armature and the

    10.____

    A. pole pieces   B. commutator
    C. bearing   D. brushes

11. If the scale on a shop drawing is 1/4 inch to the foot, then the length of a part which measures 2 3/8 inches long on the drawing is ACTUALLY _____ feet.

    11.____

    A. 9 1/2   B. 8 1/2   C. 7 1/4   D. 4 1/4

12. When welding cast iron with an oxy-acetylene torch, the BEST weld is obtained when the cast iron is

    12.____

    A. not preheated
    B. preheated slowly
    C. chilled quickly after welding
    D. chilled slowly after welding

13. A substance which can do the MOST damage to wire rope is

    13.____

    A. acid   B. grease   C. gasoline   D. oil

14. When comparing the same nominal size of extra strong iron pipe with standard iron pipe, the extra strong iron pipe has _____ diameter _____ diameter.

    14.____

    A. the same inside; but a larger outside
    B. the same outside; but a smaller inside
    C. a larger outside; and a smaller inside
    D. a larger inside; and a larger outside

15. A *Lally* column which is used in building construction consists of

    15.____

    A. a large diameter pipe fitted with a base plate at each end
    B. channels tied with lattice bars
    C. unequal sections of round pipe
    D. angles and plates

16. On a 10-24 x 7/8" screw, the number 10 indicates that the size of the outside diameter is   16._____
MOST NEARLY

    A. 0.187"   B. 10/64"   C. 10/32"   D. 0.10"

17. The liquid solution in an electrical storage battery MOST commonly is   17._____

    A. alkali   B. acid
    C. pure distilled water   D. copper sulphate

18. Manifolds on an internal combustion engine are used   18._____

    A. to mount the engine to the frame
    B. for cooling the engine
    C. in the carburetor
    D. to conduct gases into and out of the engine

19. For winter servicing of a gasoline engine, it is BEST to use an oil that   19._____

    A. has a low SAE number
    B. has a high SAE number
    C. has a very heavy consistency
    D. contains few additive detergents

20. To remove a slotted collar having internal threads from a shaft, the BEST of the following   20._____
wrenches to use is a(n) _____ wrench.

    A. Allen   B. Stillson   C. socket   D. spanner

21. When using a heavy jack placed on the ground to raise a heavy load, it is important to   21._____
place a sturdy, flat board under the jack PRIMARILY in order to

    A. facilitate placing the jack under the load
    B. reduce the jacking effort
    C. prevent the jack from slipping out from under the load
    D. decrease the jacking height

22. The pulley wheels of a block and tackle are COMMONLY called   22._____

    A. stocks   B. swivels   C. sheaves   D. guides

23. If the diameter of a machined part must be 1.035 ± 0.003", then it is ACCEPTABLE if it   23._____
measures

    A. 1.031"   B. 1.032"   C. 1.039"   D. 1.335"

24. The type of threads for ordinary screws are USUALLY the _____ type.   24._____

    A. square   B. buttress   C. V   D. Acme

25. Lead is NORMALLY used in caulking _____ pipe.   25._____

    A. copper   B. brass
    C. steel   D. cast iron

26. Of the following materials, the one which is COMMONLY used as a lubricant is

    A. powdered iron oxide
    B. powdered graphite
    C. casein
    D. rosin flux

26.____

27. On grinders, the tool rest is generally 1/8-inch from the face of the wheel.
    When dressing small parts on grinders, greater clearance is usually undesirable, because too much clearance may cause

    A. the work piece to jam and break the wheel
    B. material from the work piece to be ground off too rapidly
    C. the cutting action of the grinder to be hidden from view
    D. scoring of the wheel

27.____

28. The BEST way to determine whether the locknuts on terminals in an electrical terminal box have become loose is to

    A. use an electric tester
    B. try to tighten the nuts with an appropriate wrench
    C. tap the nuts with an insulated handle
    D. try to loosen the nuts with a pair of pliers

28.____

29. It is necessary to pour a new concrete floor for a shop. If the dimensions of the concrete slab for the floor are to be 27' x 18' x 6", then the number of cubic yards of concrete that must be poured is

    A. 9
    B. 16
    C. 54
    D. 243

29.____

30. The jaws of a vise move 1/4" for each complete turn of the handle.
    The number of complete turns necessary to open the jaws 2 3/4" is

    A. 9
    B. 10
    C. 11
    D. 12

30.____

31. The sum of 5'6", 7'3", 9' 3 1/2", and 3' 7 1/4" is

    A. 19' 8 1/2"
    B. 22' 1/2"
    C. 25' 7 3/4"
    D. 28' 8 3/4"

31.____

32. Of the following statements describing the use of carbon dioxide type fire extinguishers, the one which is TRUE is that they

    A. may be used on grease fires
    B. should not be used to extinguish electrical fires
    C. can not be used on most types of fires
    D. are ideal for use in poorly ventilated areas

32.____

33. The PRIMARY reason for a twist drill *splitting up the center* is that the

    A. cutting edges were ground at different angles
    B. lips were ground at different lengths
    C. lip clearance angle was too great
    D. lip clearance angle was insufficient

33.____

34. The PROPER file a machinist should use for finishing ordinary flat surfaces is the _____ file.

    A. Pillar
    B. Warding
    C. Hooktooth
    D. Hand

34.____

35. An all hard saw blade should be used in a hacksaw frame when sawing   35.____

    A. tool steel   B. channel iron
    C. aluminum   D. thin wall copper tubing

36. The surface gage is generally NOT used for   36.____

    A. laying out
    B. leveling and lining up work
    C. checking angles and tapers
    D. locating centers on rough work

Questions 37-40.

DIRECTIONS: The sketch shown below refers to a piping arrangement for connecting a new space heater. Questions 37 through 40 are based on it.

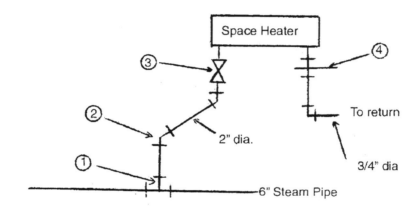

37. Pipe fitting 1 is a   37.____

    A. bull tee   B. sanitary tee
    C. reducing tee   D. cross

38. Pipe fitting 2 is a   38.____

    A. branch tee   B. Y fitting
    C. right elbow   D. 45 degree elbow

39. Pipe fitting 3 is a   39.____

    A. coupling   B. flange
    C. valve   D. steam trap

40. Pipe fitting 4 is a   40.____

    A. union   B. valve   C. tee   D. reducer

KEY (CORRECT ANSWERS)

1.	A	11.	A	21.	C	31.	C
2.	D	12.	B	22.	C	32.	A
3.	C	13.	A	23.	B	33.	D
4.	B	14.	B	24.	C	34.	D
5.	C	15.	A	25.	D	35.	A
6.	A	16.	A	26.	B	36.	C
7.	B	17.	B	27.	A	37.	C
8.	D	18.	D	28.	B	38.	D
9.	C	19.	A	29.	A	39.	C
10.	A	20.	D	30.	C	40.	A

———

EXAMINATION SECTION
TEST 1

DIRECTIONS: Each question or incomplete statement is followed by several suggested answers or completions. Select the one that BEST answers the question or completes the statement. *PRINT THE LETTER OF THE CORRECT ANSWER IN THE SPACE AT THE RIGHT.*

1. On an engine lathe, the saddle is a part which

    A. is attached to the tailstock
    B. rotates and holds the faceplate
    C. slides along the ways
    D. houses the back gears

1.____

2. To facilitate milling cast iron, it is BEST to use

    A. an emulsion of soluble oil and water as a lubricant
    B. an emulsion of soluble oil and water with a small percentage of soda as a lubricant
    C. lard oil as a lubricant
    D. no lubricant

2.____

3. When using a milling machine in a machine shop, a MAJOR difference of climb milling as compared to standard milling is that climb milling

    A. uses more power
    B. produces a better finish
    C. uses a downward cut
    D. uses cutters with less rake

3.____

4. In an automotive gasoline engine, the camshaft is used PRIMARILY to

    A. drive the transmission
    B. operate the valve lifters
    C. change the reciprocating motion of the pistons to rotary motion
    D. operate the choke mechanism

4.____

5. A magnetic motor starter is to be controlled with momentary start-stop pushbuttons at two locations.
The number of control wires required, respectively, in the conduit between the controller and the first station and in the conduit between the two stations is _____ and _____.

    A. 3;3   B. 4; 4   C. 3; 4   D. 2; 4

5.____

6. The type of fitting to use to join a 1 inch branch compressed air, pipe line to a 2 inch main air line is a

    A. reducing valve   B. reducing coupling
    C. reducing tee   D. street elbow

6.____

7. If steel weighs 0.30 pounds per cubic inch, then the weight of a 2 inch square steel bar 90 inches long is _____ pounds.

    A. 27   B. 54   C. 108   D. 360

7.____

8. In arc welding, the filler metal is provided PRIMARILY by   8._____

    A. the metal to be welded
    B. a second rod of filler metal
    C. the slag
    D. the electrode

9. Oil or grease should NOT be applied to the oxygen valve of an oxyacetylene torch PRI-   9._____
MARILY because this can

    A. produce an explosion hazard
    B. corrode the valve
    C. give an incorrect pressure reading
    D. make the valve too slippery to handle

10. The PRIMARY function of the thermostat in the cooling system of an automobile engine   10._____
is to

    A. control the operating temperature of the engine
    B. keep the operating temperature of the engine as low as possible
    C. provide the proper amount of heat for the heater
    D. retain engine heat when the engine gets hot

11. The PRIMARY purpose of the condenser in the ignition circuit of a gasoline engine is to   11._____

    A. boost the ignition voltage
    B. rectify the ignition voltage
    C. adjust the coil voltage
    D. reduce arcing at the distributor breaker points

12. The PRIMARY purpose of the differential in the rear drive train of an automotive vehicle   12._____
is to allow each of the rear wheels to

    A. rotate at different speeds
    B. go in reverse
    C. rotate with maximum torque
    D. absorb road shocks

13. When grinding a fillet weld smooth, it is best NOT to grind   13._____

    A. after the weld has cooled off
    B. slowly
    C. too much of the weld material away
    D. the surface smooth

14. When using a hand file to finish a round piece of wood rod held between lathe centers, it   14._____
is usually BEST to

    A. hold the file handle with one hand and to guide the file with the other hand
    B. use the file with the lathe not rotating
    C. hold the file with one hand and guide the workpiece with the other hand
    D. use a file without a handle

15. If the voltage on a 3-phase squirrel case induction motor is reduced to 90% of its rating, the starting current 15.____

    A. increases slightly
    B. is unchanged
    C. decreases 10%
    D. decreases 20%

16. If the voltage on a 3-phase squirrel case induction motor is reduced to 90% of its rating, the full load current 16.____

    A. decreases slightly
    B. is unchanged
    C. increases 10%
    D. increases 20%

17. When laying brick, the PRIMARY reason for wetting the brick before laying it is that 17.____

    A. the brick will absorb less water from the mortar and form a better bond
    B. wet bricks are easier to position
    C. wet bricks take less time to form a bond to mortar
    D. less cement is needed in the mortar

18. Concrete is a mixture that NORMALLY consists of cement, 18.____

    A. sand, and water
    B. sand, mortar, and water
    C. gravel, and water
    D. sand, gravel, and water

19. A type of rivet which can be put in place even when a worker does NOT have access to the back side of the work is known as a _____ rivet. 19.____

    A. *bucking*
    B. *double-head*
    C. *pop*
    D. *side*

20. The fraction which is equal to 0.875 is 20.____

    A. 7/16   B. 5/8   C. 3/4   D. 7/8

21. When fabricating forms for pouring concrete, the MAIN advantage of using plywood sheets over sheets made of pine boards is that plywood 21.____

    A. doesn't splinter
    B. is lighter
    C. is less expensive
    D. resists warping better

22. When chipping concrete with a pneumatic hammer, the MOST important safety item that a man should wear is 22.____

    A. goggles
    B. gloves
    C. a hard hat
    D. rubber boots

23. It is considered POOR practice to paint a wooden ladder PRIMARILY because the 23.____

    A. paint will wear off in time
    B. rails will become susceptible to damage
    C. paint will shorten the life of the rungs
    D. paint can hide serious defects

24. A concrete wall is 36' long, 9' high, and 1 1/2' thick. The number of cubic yards of concrete that were needed to make this wall is 24.____

    A. 14   B. 18   C. 27   D. 36

25. Before disassembling a complex mechanical machine, a mechanic may use a center   25._____
punch to make adjacent punch marks on two or more of the parts in the machine in order
to

    A. mark each part as he removes it
    B. check the hardness of the parts
    C. loosen the parts
    D. give himself a guide for correct reassembly

26. From among the following tools, the BEST one to use in cutting off a section of 4-inch   26._____
cast iron pipe would be a

    A. hammer and chisel   B. pneumatic hammer
    C. hammer and star drill   D. hacksaw

27. The MOST important reason for removing pressure from an air hose before breaking a   27._____
hose connection is to avoid

    A. damage to the air compressor
    B. losing air
    C. damage to the hose connection
    D. personal injury

28. When using a rope fall to lower a heavy load vertically, the strain on the hand line can be   28._____
reduced and the load lowered more safely if the

    A. rope is wound three or four times around a fixed post
    B. rope is lightly greased
    C. rope is held very tightly in the sheaves of the fall
    D. sheaves of the fall are small in diameter

29. Oil is frequently applied to the inside of forms prior to pouring concrete in them in order to   29._____

    A. make the concrete flow better
    B. make stripping easier
    C. keep the moisture in the concrete
    D. protect the forms

30. The instrument generally used to determine the specific gravity of a lead-acid storage   30._____
battery is the

    A. ammeter   B. voltmeter   C. ohmmeter   D. hydrometer

31. A tachometer is an instrument that is used to measure   31._____

    A. horizontal distances
    B. radial distances
    C. current in electric circuits
    D. motor speed

32. If the centers of a lathe are out of line when turning a cylindrical piece, it will cause   32._____

    A. the centers to be damaged
    B. a spiral groove to be cut on the piece

C. the cutting tool to be damaged
D. the piece to have a taper

33. A low reading on the oil pressure gauge of a gasoline engine may mean that the   33.____

    A. engine bearings are too tight
    B. crankcase oil level is too low
    C. transmission oil level is too low
    D. transmission oil needs changing

34. Although cloth tapes are used for taking measurements in many kinds of work, they   34.____
    should NOT be used when taking accurate measurements PRIMARILY because

    A. small changes in the amount of pull on these tapes can make a big difference in
       the reading
    B. the numbers become worn easily and are thus difficult to read
    C. small temperature changes cause large changes in readings
    D. there are too few subdivisions of each inch on these tapes

35. When painting walls with two coats of paint, a different color is used for each coat PRI-   35.____
    MARILY to

    A. check for full coverage by the second coat
    B. provide a better appearance
    C. lower the painting cost
    D. allow the painter to use any color paint for the first coat

36. To drill a hole in the same place on a number of identical steel parts, it is BEST to use a   36.____

    A. blanking tool   B. punch press
    C. counterbore   D. jig

37. The MAIN purpose of a chuck on a lathe is to   37.____

    A. hold the workpiece
    B. hold the cutting tool
    C. allow speed changes to be made
    D. allow screw threads to be turned

38. The metal which has the GREATEST resistance to the flow of electricity is   38.____

    A. steel   B. copper   C. silver   D. gold

39. Tinning a soldering iron means   39.____

    A. applying flux to the tip
    B. cleaning the tip to make it bright
    C. applying a coat of solder to the tip
    D. heating the iron to the proper temperature

40. A protractor is an instrument that is used to   40.____

    A. measure the thickness of shims
    B. drill blind holes
    C. measure angles
    D. drill tapped holes

KEY (CORRECT ANSWERS)

1.	C	11.	D	21.	D	31.	D
2.	D	12.	A	22.	A	32.	D
3.	C	13.	C	23.	D	33.	B
4.	B	14.	A	24.	B	34.	A
5.	C	15.	C	25.	D	35.	A
6.	C	16.	C	26.	A	36.	D
7.	C	17.	A	27.	D	37.	A
8.	D	18.	D	28.	A	38.	A
9.	A	19.	C	29.	B	39.	C
10.	A	20.	D	30.	D	40.	C

TEST 2

DIRECTIONS: Each question or incomplete statement is followed by several suggested answers or completions. Select the one that BEST answers the question or completes the statement. *PRINT THE LETTER OF THE CORRECT ANSWER IN THE SPACE AT THE RIGHT.*

1. Common nail sizes are designated by
   - A. penny size
   - B. weight
   - C. head size
   - D. shank diameter

   1.____

2. Toggle bolts should be used to fasten conduit clamps to a _____ wall.
   - A. concrete
   - B. hollow tile
   - C. brick
   - D. solid masonry

   2.____

3. Backlash in a pair of meshed gears is defined as the
   - A. distance between the gear centers
   - B. gear ratio of the pair
   - C. wear of the teeth
   - D. *play* between the gear teeth

   3.____

4. Relief valves on an air supply reservoir are used for the purpose of
   - A. protecting the reservoir against excessively high pressures
   - B. compensating for air leakage from the reservoir
   - C. retaining the air in the reservoir
   - D. draining moisture from the reservoir

   4.____

5. Of the following, the BEST tool to use for securely tightening a one-inch standard hexagonal nut is a(n)
   - A. monkey wrench
   - B. open-end wrench
   - C. Stillson wrench
   - D. pair of heavy duty pliers

   5.____

6. The type of pipe which is MOST likely to be broken by careless handling is one made of
   - A. copper
   - B. steel
   - C. brass
   - D. cast iron

   6.____

7. Open-end wrenches are usually made with the sides of the jaws at about a 15 degree angle to the centerline of the handle.
   The PURPOSE of this type of design is that it
   - A. increases the leverage of the wrench
   - B. enables the wrench to lock on to the bolt head
   - C. is useful when using the wrench in close quarters
   - D. prevents extending the handle with a piece of pipe

   7.____

8. The type of tool which is used with a portable electric drill to cut 2-inch diameter circular holes in wood is the
   - A. reamer
   - B. twist drill
   - C. hole saw
   - D. circular saw

   8.____

9. For a certain job, you will need 25 steel bars 1 inch in diameter and 4'6" long. 9.____
If these bars weigh 3 pounds per foot of length, then the TOTAL weight for all 25 bars
is _____ pounds.

   A. 13.5   B. 75.0   C. 112.5   D. 337.5

10. If the allowable load on a wooden scaffold is 60 pounds per square foot and the scaffold 10.____
surface area is 3 feet by 12 feet, then the MAXIMUM total distributed load that is permitted on the scaffold is _____ pounds.

   A. 720   B. 1800   C. 2160   D. 2400

11. If the floor area of one shop is 15' by 21'3" and the size of an adjacent shop is 18' by 11.____
30'6", then the TOTAL floor area of these two shops is _____ square feet.

   A. 1127.75   B. 867.75   C. 549.0   D. 318.75

12. To make certain that two points separated by a vertical distance of 8 feet are in exact ver- 12.____
tical alignment, it would be BEST to use a

   A. plumb bob   B. spirit level
   C. protractor   D. mason's line

13. An offset screwdriver is MOST useful for turning a wood screw when 13.____

   A. the screw is large
   B. space above the screw is limited
   C. the screw is the Phillips type
   D. the screw must be tightened very securely

14. If an 8-32 x 11" machine screw is not available, the screw which could MOST easily be 14.____
modified to use in an emergency is the

   A. 8-36 x 1"   B. 10-32 x 1"
   C. 6-32 x 1 1/2"   D. 8-32 x 1 1/2"

15. After a file has been used on soft material, the BEST way to clean the file is to use 15.____

   A. a file card   B. fine emery cloth
   C. a bench brush   D. a cleaning solution

16. The type of wrench that should be used to tighten a nut or bolt to a specified number of 16.____
foot-pounds is a _____ wrench.

   A. torque   B. spanner   C. box   D. lug

17. When a hacksaw blade is turned at right angles to its holding frame, it is done PRIMA- 17.____
RILY to

   A. increase the accuracy of cutting
   B. reduce the strain on the frame
   C. cut more rapidly
   D. make cuts which are deeper than the frame

18. The PRIMARY purpose of galvanizing steel is to 18.____

   A. increase the strength of the steel
   B. provide a good base for painting

C. prevent rusting of the steel
D. improve the appearance of the steel

19. When installing a heavy new machine in a shop, the BEST way to level the machine on the shop floor is to

    A. use steel shims under the feet
    B. use a thin layer of cement under the feet
    C. grind the feet of the machine to suit
    D. install adjustable shock mounts

19.____

20. The type of valve that permits fluid to flow in one direction ONLY in a pipe run is a _____ valve.

    A. check   B. gate   C. globe   D. cross

20.____

21. If the scale on a shop drawing is 1/2 inch to the foot, then the length of a part which measures 4 1/4 inches long on the drawing has a length of APPROXIMATELY _____ feet.

    A. 2 1/8   B. 4 1/4   C. 8 1/2   D. 10 3/4

21.____

22. It is important to use safety shoes PRIMARILY to guard the feet against

    A. tripping hazards   B. heavy falling objects
    C. shock hazards   D. mud and dirt

22.____

23. When using a wrench to tighten a bolt, it is considered BAD practice to extend the handle of the wrench with a pipe for added leverage PRIMARILY because

    A. the pipe may break
    B. the bolt head may be broken off
    C. more space will be needed to turn the wrench with the pipe on it
    D. no increase in leverage is obtained in this manner

23.____

24. To accurately measure the small gap between relay contacts, it is BEST to use a(n)

    A. depth gauge   B. GO-NO GO gauge
    C. feeler gauge   D. inside caliper

24.____

25. The plumbing symbol shown on the right represents a
    A. steam trap
    B. coupling
    C. cross fitting
    D. valve

25.____

26. On oxyacetylene welding equipment, the feed pressure of the gases is reduced by means of

    A. tip valves   B. regulator valves
    C. relief valves   D. nozzle size

26.____

27. The purpose of the ignition coil in a gasoline engine is PRIMARILY to

    A. smooth the voltage   B. raise the voltage
    C. raise the current   D. smooth the current

27.____

28. The weight per foot of length of a 2" x 2" square steel bar as compared to a 1" x 1" square steel bar is _____ times as much. 28.____

    A. two   B. four   C. six   D. eight

29. Electric arc welding is COMMONLY done using _____ amperage and _____ voltage. 29.____

    A. low; low   B. low; high
    C. high; low   D. high; high

30. Creosote is COMMONLY used 30.____

    A. to preserve wood
    B. to produce a good finish on wood
    C. as a primer coat of paint on wood
    D. to fireproof wood

31. The term *shipping* when applied to rope means 31.____

    A. coiling the rope in a tight ball
    B. lubricating the strands with tallow
    C. wetting the rope with water to make it easier to coil
    D. binding the ends with cord to prevent unraveling

32. Many portable electric power tools, such as electric drills, which operate on 110V A.C., have a third conductor in the power cord.
The reason for this extra conductor is to 32.____

    A. prevent overheating of the power cord
    B. provide a spare conductor
    C. make the power cord stronger
    D. ground the case of the tool

33. The sum of 4 feet 3 1/4 inches, 7 feet 2 1/2 inches, and 11 feet 1/4 inch is _____ feet _____ inches. 33.____

    A. 21; 6 1/4   B. 22; 6   C. 23; 5   D. 24; 5 3/4

34. The number 0.038 is read as 34.____

    A. 38 tenths   B. 38 hundredths
    C. 38 thousandths   D. 38 ten-thousandths

35. Assume that an employee is paid at the rate of $5.43 per hour with time and a half for overtime past 40 hours in a week.
If he works 43 hours in a week, his gross weekly pay is 35.____

    A. $217.20   B. $219.20   C. $229.59   D. $241.64

36. Vapor lock in a vehicle with a gasoline engine is caused by excessive heat.
To prevent vapor lock, it may be necessary to relocate the(a) 36.____

    A. ignition system   B. cooling system
    C. starter motor   D. part of the fuel line

37. An ohmmeter is an instrument for measuring electrical 37.____

    A. voltage   B. current   C. power   D. resistance

38. A thermal overload device on a motor is used to protect it against   38.____

    A. high voltage
    B. over-speeding
    C. excessively high current
    D. low temperatures

39. A union is a pipe fitting that is used to join together   39.____

    A. two pipes of different diameters
    B. two pipes of the same diameter
    C. a threaded pipe to a sweated pipe
    D. two sweated pipes of the same diameter

40. If a 30 ampere fuse is placed in a fuse box for a circuit requiring a 15 ampere fuse,   40.____

    A. serious damage to the circuit may result from an overload
    B. better protection will be provided for the circuit
    C. the larger fuse will tend to blow more often since it carries more current
    D. it will eliminate maintenance problems

KEY (CORRECT ANSWERS)

1.	A	11.	B	21.	C	31.	D
2.	B	12.	A	22.	B	32.	D
3.	D	13.	B	23.	B	33.	B
4.	A	14.	D	24.	C	34.	C
5.	B	15.	A	25.	D	35.	D
6.	D	16.	A	26.	B	36.	D
7.	C	17.	D	27.	B	37.	D
8.	C	18.	C	28.	B	38.	C
9.	D	19.	A	29.	C	39.	B
10.	C	20.	A	30.	A	40.	A

EXAMINATION SECTION
TEST 1

DIRECTIONS: Each question or incomplete statement is followed by several suggested answers or completions. Select the one that BEST answers the question or completes the statement. *PRINT THE LETTER OF THE CORRECT ANSWER IN THE SPACE AT THE RIGHT.*

1. The process of determining the quantity of goods and materials that are in stock is commonly called

    A. receiving   B. disbursement
    C. reconciliation   D. inventory

    1.____

2. Proper and effective storage procedure involves the storing of

    A. items together on the basis of class grouping
    B. all items in chronological order based on date received
    C. items in alphabetical order based on date of delivery
    D. items randomly wherever space is available

    2.____

3. Which of the following is the FIRST step involved in correctly taking an inventory?

    A. Reconciliation of inventory records with the number of items on hand
    B. Analysis of possible discrepancies between items on hand and the stock record balance
    C. Identification and recording of the locations of all items in stock
    D. Issuance of an inventory directive to all vendors

    3.____

4. Supply items other than food which are subject to deterioration should be checked

    A. at delivery time only   B. occasionally
    C. only when issued   D. periodically

    4.____

5. For which of the following supplies is it MOST necessary to provide ample ventilation?

    A. Small rubber parts   B. Metal products
    C. Flammable liquids   D. Wooden items

    5.____

6. Storing small lots of supplies in an area designated for the storage of large lots of supplies will generally result in

    A. *loss* of supplies   B. *loss* of storage space
    C. *increase* in inventory   D. *increase* in storage space

    6.____

7. Compliance with fire preventive measures is a major requirement for the maintenance of a safe warehouse. Which of the following statements is LEAST important in describing a measure useful in maintaining a fire preventive facility?

    A. Smoking is only permitted in designated areas.
    B. Oil-soaked rags should be disposed of promptly and not stored.
    C. When not in use, electrical machinery should be grounded.
    D. Gasoline-powered materials handling equipment should not be refueled with the motor running.

    7.____

8. It is POOR storage practice to store small valuable items loosely in open containers in bulk storage areas because doing so results in the

    8.____

    A. misplacement of such items
    B. pilferage of these items
    C. deterioration of such supplies
    D. hindrance in inspection of these supplies

9. Assume that you have been placed in charge of the receiving operations at your garage. Generally, you receive all the supplies you order during the first week of each month. Of the following, the MOST effective and economic way to facilitate receiving operations would be to

    9.____

    A. secure overtime authorization for laborers during that week
    B. have all truck deliveries made in one day
    C. stagger truck deliveries throughout each morning of the week
    D. assign all personnel to receiving duty for that week

10. Effective security measures must be instituted to provide for the safekeeping of city supplies.
However, the scope and complexity of security measures used at a warehouse facility should correspond MOST NEARLY to the

    10.____

    A. value of supplies stored in the warehouse
    B. borough in which the warehouse is located
    C. level of warehouse activity
    D. age of the warehouse facility

11. To facilitate handling and issuance of supply items that have a high turnover rate, they should generally be stored

    11.____

    A. away from accessible aisles
    B. on upper shelves
    C. in a locked compartment area
    D. close to the service counter area

12. The MOST important factor to be considered in effectively storing heavy, bulky, and difficult-to-handle items is to store these items

    12.____

    A. as close to shipping areas as possible
    B. in storage areas with a low floor-load capacity
    C. only in outside storage sheds
    D. away from aisles

Questions 13-16.

DIRECTIONS: Questions 13 through 16 are to be answered using ONLY the information in the following passage.

Fire exit drills should be established and held periodically to effectively train personnel to leave their working area promptly upon proper signal and to evacuate the building speedily but without confusion. All fire exit drills should be carefully planned and carried out in a serious manner under rigid discipline so as to provide positive protection in the event of a real emergency. As a general rule, the local fire department should be furnished advance information regarding the exact date and time the exit drill is scheduled. When it is impossible to hold regular drills, written instructions should be distributed to all employees.

Depending upon individual circumstances, fires in warehouses vary from those of fast development that are almost instantly beyond any possibility of employee control to others of relatively slow development where a small readily attackable flame may be present for periods of time up to 15 minutes or more during which simple attack with fire extinguishers or small building hoses may prevent the fire development. In any case, it is characteristic of many warehouse fires that at a certain point in development they flash up to the top of the stack, increase heat quickly, and spread rapidly. There is a degree of inherent danger in attacking warehouse type fires and all employees should be thoroughly trained in the use of the types of extinguishers or small hoses in the buildings and well instructed in the necessity of always staying between the fire and a direct pass to an exit.

13. Employees should be instructed that, when fighting a fire, they MUST   13._____

    A. try to control the blaze
    B. extinguish any fire in 15 minutes
    C. remain between the fire and a direct passage to the exit
    D. keep the fire between themselves and the fire exit

14. Whenever conditions are such that regular fire drills cannot be held, then which one of   14._____
the following actions should be taken?

    A. The local fire department should be notified.
    B. Rigid discipline should be maintained during work hours.
    C. Personnel should be instructed to leave their working area by whatever means are available.
    D. Employees should receive fire drill procedures in writing.

15. The passage indicates that the purpose of fire exit drills is to train employees to   15._____

    A. control a fire before it becomes uncontrollable
    B. act as firefighters
    C. leave the working area promptly
    D. be serious

16. According to the passage, fire exit drills will prove to be of *utmost* effectiveness if   16._____

    A. employee participation is made voluntary
    B. they take place periodically
    C. the fire department actively participates
    D. they are held without advance planning

Questions 17-20.

DIRECTIONS: Questions 17 through 20 are to be answered using ONLY the information in the following paragraph.

A report is frequently ineffective because the person writing it is not fully acquainted with all the necessary details before he actually starts to construct the report. All details pertaining to the subject should be known before the report is started. If the essential facts are not known, they should be investigated. It is wise to have essential facts written down rather than to depend too much on memory, especially if the facts pertain to such matters as amounts, dates, names of persons, or other specific data. When the necessary information has been gathered, the general plan and content of the report should be thought out before the writing is actually begun. A person with little or no experience in writing reports may find that it is wise to make a brief outline. Persons with more experience should not need a written outline, but they should make mental notes of the steps they are to follow. If writing reports without dictation is a regular part of an office worker's duties, he should set aside a certain time during the day when he is least likely to be interrupted. That may be difficult, but in most offices there are certain times in the day when the callers, telephone calls, and other interruptions are not numerous. During those times, it is best to write reports that need undivided concentration. Reports that are written amid a series of interruptions may be poorly done.

17.   Before starting to write an effective report, it is necessary to   17._____

    A.   memorize all specific information
    B.   disregard ambiguous data
    C.   know all pertinent information
    D.   develop a general plan

18.   Reports dealing with complex and difficult material should be   18._____

    A.   prepared and written by the supervisor of the unit
    B.   written when there is the least chance of interruption
    C.   prepared and written as part of regular office routine
    D.   outlined and then dictated

19.   According to the passage, employees with no prior familiarity in writing reports may find it   19._____
helpful to

    A.   prepare a brief outline
    B.   mentally prepare a synopsis of the report's content
    C.   have a fellow employee help in writing the report
    D.   consult previous reports

20.   In writing a report, needed information which is unclear should be   20._____

    A.   disregarded   B.   investigated
    C.   memorized   D.   gathered

KEY (CORRECT ANSWERS)

1.	D		11.	D
2.	A		12.	A
3.	C		13.	C
4.	D		14.	D
5.	C		15.	C
6.	B		16.	B
7.	C		17.	C
8.	B		18.	B
9.	C		19.	A
10.	A		20.	B

TEST 2

DIRECTIONS: Each question or incomplete statement is followed by several suggested answers or completions. Select the one that BEST answers the question or completes the statement. *PRINT THE LETTER OF THE CORRECT ANSWER IN THE SPACE AT THE RIGHT.*

Questions 1-4.

DIRECTIONS: Questions 1 through 4 are to be answered using ONLY the information in the following passage.

The operation and maintenance of the stock-location system is a warehousing function and responsibility. The stock locator system shall consist of a file of stock-location record cards, either manually or mechanically prepared, depending upon the equipment available. The file shall contain an individual card for each stock item stored in the depot, with the records maintained in stock number sequence.

The locator file is used for all receiving, warehousing, inventory, and shipping activities in the depot. The locator file must contain complete and accurate data to provide ready support to the various depot functions and activities, i.e., processing shipping documents, updating records on mechanized equipment, where applicable, supplying accurate locator information for stock selection and proper storage of receipts, consolidating storage locations of identical items not subject to shelf-life control, and preventing the consolidation of stock of limited shelf-life items. The file is also essential in accomplishing location surveys and the inventory program.

Storage of bulk stock items by "spot-location" method is generally recognized as the best means of obtaining maximum warehouse space utilization. Despite the fact that the spot-location method of storage enables full utilization of storage capacity, this method may prove inefficient unless it is supplemented by adequate stock-location control, including proper lay-out and accurate maintenance of stock locator cards.

1. The manner in which the stock-location record cards should be filed is   1.____

    A. alphabetically   B. chronologically
    C. numerically   D. randomly

2. Items of limited shelf-life should   2.____

    A. not be stored
    B. not be stored together
    C. be stored in stock sequence
    D. be stored together

3. Which one of the following is NOT mentioned in the passage as a use of the stock-location system?   3.____
   Aids in

    A. accomplishing location surveys
    B. providing information for stock selection
    C. storing items received for the first time
    D. processing shipping documents

4. If the spot-location method of storing is used, then the use of the stock-location system is   4.____

    A. *desirable,* because the stock-location system is recognized as the best means of obtaining maximum warehouse space utilization
    B. *undesirable,* because additional records must be kept
    C. *desirable,* because stock-location controls are necessary with the spot-location storage method
    D. *undesirable,* because a stock-locator system will take up valuable storage space

Questions 5-8.

DIRECTIONS: Questions 5 through 8 are to be answered using ONLY the information in the following paragraph.

Known damage is defined as damage that is apparent and acknowledged by the carrier at the time of delivery to the purchaser. A meticulous inspection of the damaged goods should be completed by the purchaser and a notation specifying the extent of the damage should be applied to the carrier's original freight bill. As is the case in known loss, it is necessary for the carrier's agent to acknowledge by signature the damage notation in order for it to have any legal status. The purchaser should not refuse damaged freight since it is his legal duty to accept the property and to employ every available and reasonable means to protect the shipment and minimize the loss. Acceptance of a damaged shipment does not endanger any legitimate claim the purchaser may have against the carrier for damage. If the purchaser fails to observe the legal duty to accept damaged freight, the carrier may consider it abandoned. After properly notifying the vendor and purchaser of his intentions, the carrier may dispose of the material at public sale.

5. Before disposing of an abandoned shipment, the carrier must   5.____

    A. notify the vendor and the carrier's agent
    B. advise the vendor and purchaser of his plans
    C. notify the purchaser and the carrier's agent
    D. obtain the signature of the carrier's agent on the freight bill

6. In the case of damaged freight, the original freight bill will only have legal value if it is   6.____
signed by the

    A. carrier's agent   B. purchaser
    C. vendor   D. purchaser and vendor

7. A purchaser does not protect a shipment of cargo that is damaged and is further deterio-   7.____
rating.
According to the above paragraph, the action of the purchaser is

    A. *acceptable,* because he is not obligated to protect damaged cargo
    B. *unacceptable,* because damaged cargo must be protected no matter what is involved
    C. *acceptable,* because he took possession of the cargo
    D. *unacceptable,* because he is obligated by law to protect the cargo

8. The TWO requirements that must be satisfied before cargo can be labeled *known dam-*   8.____
   age are signs of evident damage and

   A. confirmation by the carrier or carrier's agent that this is so
   B. delayed shipment of goods
   C. signature of acceptance by the purchaser
   D. acknowledgment by the vendor that this is so

Questions 9-13.

DIRECTIONS: Questions 9 through 13 are to be answered on the basis of the following graph.

GARBAGE COLLECTIONS MADE JAN. 1 - DEC. 31, IN TONS (SHORT TON)

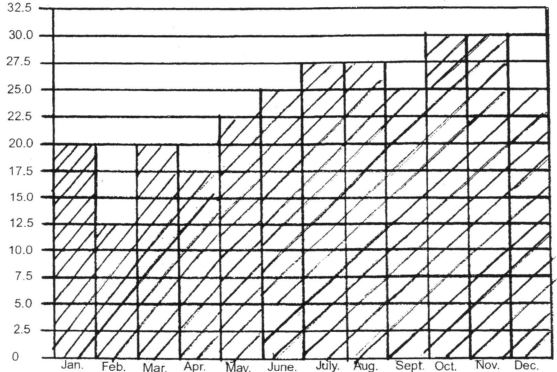

9. According to the information presented in the graph, the weight of the average monthly   9.____
   collection of garbage is
   MOST NEARLY _____ tons.

   A. 22.5   B. 23.5   C. 24.5   D. 25.5

10. If a truck can carry 6,000 lbs., then the number of truck-loads collected during the year   10.____
    was MOST NEARLY

   A. 55   B. 75   C. 95   D. 115

11. The amount of garbage collected during the second half of the year represents   11.____
    APPROXIMATELY what percentage of the total garbage collected during the year?

   A. 50%   B. 60%   C. 70%   D. 80%

12. During the months of September, October, and November, approximately 12% of the col-   12.____
lections consisted of fallen leaves.
What was the weight of the remaining garbage NOT containing fallen leaves for that
period?
_____ tons.

   A. 10   B. 20   C. 65   D. 75

13. Assume that the collections for the year as shown in the above graph exceeded the pre-   13.____
vious year's collection by 17%. The collection made in the previous year was MOST
NEARLY _____ tons.

   A. 50   B. 225   C. 240   D. 275 .

Questions 14-17.

DIRECTIONS: Questions 14 through 17 are to be answered on the basis of the following
graph

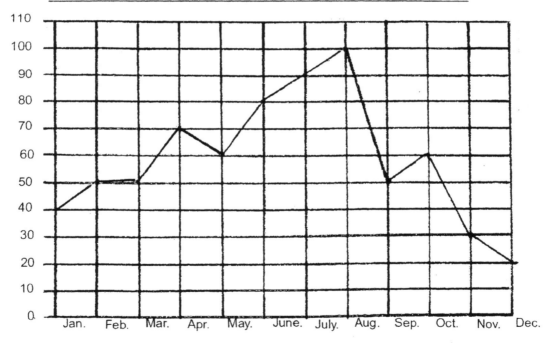

INVENTORY LEVELS (IN DOZENS) OF ITEM A IN STOREHOUSE
AT BEGINNING OF MONTH FOR A PERIOD OF TWELVS MONTH

14. The average monthly inventory level during the course of the year was MOST NEARLY   14.____
_____ dozen.

   A. 45   B. 60   C. 75   D. 90

15. If one dozen items fit in a carton measuring 2 feet by 2 feet by 3 feet, what MINIMUM vol-   15.____
ume would be required to store the maximum August inventory?
_____ cubic feet.

   A. 12   B. 100   C. 700   D. 1,200

16. Assume that deliveries are made to the storehouse on the first working day of each month. If 30% of the June inventory was consumed during the month, how many items had to be delivered to reach the July inventory level? _____ items.   16.____

    A. 288   B. 408   C. 696   D. 1,080

17. Which three-month period contained the LOWEST average inventory level?   17.____

    A. Jan., Feb., March   B. April, May, June
    C. July, Aug., Sept.   D. Oct., Nov., Dec.

18. Assume that it takes approximately 1 1/2 minutes to unload a dozen identical items from a delivery truck.
    At this speed, the amount of time it should take to unload a shipment of 876 items is MOST NEARLY _____ minutes.   18.____

    A. 90   B. 100   C. 110   D. 120

19. Assume that a shop clerk has received a bill of $108 for a delivery of clamps which cost $4.32 per dozen.
    How many clamps should there be in this delivery?   19.____

    A. 25   B. 36   C. 300   D. 360

20. Employee A has not used any leave time and has accumulated a total of 45 leave days. How many months did it take Employee A to have accumulated 45 leave days if the accrual rate is 1 2/3 days per month?   20.____

    A. 25   B. 27   C. 29   D. 31

_____

KEY (CORRECT ANSWERS)

1. C		11. B
2. B		12. D
3. C		13. C
4. C		14. B
5. B		15. D
6. A		16. B
7. D		17. D
8. A		18. C
9. B		19. C
10. C		20. B

ARITHMETICAL REASONING
EXAMINATION SECTION
TEST 1

DIRECTIONS: Each question or incomplete statement is followed by several suggested answers or completions. Select the one that BEST answers the question or completes the statement. *PRINT THE LETTER OF THE CORRECT ANSWER IN THE SPACE AT THE RIGHT.*

1. The sum of the fractions 3/32, 3/16, 3/8, and 3/4 is equal to   1.____

    A. 1 13/32   B. 1 5/16   C. 1 7/8   D. 3

2. If a maintainer earns $11.52 per hour, and time and one-half for overtime, his gross salary for a week in which he works 5 hours over his regular 40 hours should be   2.____

    A. $460.80   B. $518.80   C. $547.20   D. $578.80

3. If the diameter of a shaft must be 2.620 inches plus or minus .002 inches, the shaft will be SATISFACTORY if it has a diameter of _____ inches.   3.____

    A. 2.518   B. 2.600   C. 2.617   D. 2.621

4. A bus part costs $275 per 100 when purchased from a vendor. The bus part could be made in the bus machine shop at a labor cost of $60 for 50 units, with material and other costs amounting to $25 for 25 units.
If 100 such parts were made in the bus shop, there would be a saving of   4.____

    A. $55   B. $95   C. $140   D. $165

5. The sum of 9/16", 11/32", 15/64", and 1 3/32" is MOST NEARLY   5.____

    A. 2.234"   B. 2.134"   C. 2.334"   D. 2.214"

6. The diameter of a circle whose circumference is 14.5" is MOST NEARLY   6.____

    A. 4.62"   B. 4.81"   C. 4.72"   D. 4.51"

7. A bus part cost $90 per 100 when purchased from a vendor. The bus part could be made in the bus machine shop at a labor cost of $20 for 50 units and material and other costs amounting to $10 for 25 units.
If 100 such parts are made in the bus shop, there would be a saving of   7.____

    A. $10   B. $30   C. $40   D. $60

8. A bus storage battery having a 300 ampere-hour capacity is 50% discharged.
If the bus running schedule for the day is such that the battery will be charging at an average rate of 30 amperes for 2 1/2 hours and discharging at an average rate of 9 amperes for 5 hours, then at the end of the day, the battery will be APPROXIMATELY   8.____

    A. at full charge   B. 75% charged
    C. 60% charged   D. 50% charged

9. If the total time allowance for replacing the glass in a broken bus window is 75 minutes, how many jobs of this kind would a maintainer be expected to do in 40 hours of work?

9.____

    A. 32   B. 40   C. 60   D. 72

10. A certain rod is tapered so that it changes diameter at a rate of 1/4 inch per foot of length. If the tapered rod is 3 inches long, then the difference in diameter between the two ends is MOST NEARLY

10.____

    A. 0.250"   B. 0.187"   C. 0.135"   D. 0.062"

11. How many 9 1/2 inch long pieces of copper tubing can be cut from a 20-foot length of tubing?

11.____

    A. 24   B. 25   C. 26   D. 27

12. Two splice plates must be cut from a piece of sheet steel that has an overall length of 14 3/8 inches. The plates are to be 7 5/8 inches and 5 1/4 inches long.
If 1/16 inch is allowed for each saw cut, then how much material would be left?

12.____

    A. 1 3/8"   B. I 1/2"   C. 1 5/8"   D. 1 3/4"

13. A maintainer requires several lengths of tubing for oil lines as follows: 12 7/16 inches, 14 5/16 inches, 9 3/16 inches, 9 1/8 inches, 6 1/4 inches, and 5 inches.
The TOTAL length of tubing required is MOST NEARLY _____, feet.

13.____

    A. 2   B. 3   C. 4   D. 5

14. Two-thirds of 10 feet is MOST NEARLY

14.____

    A. 6'2"   B. 6'8"   C. 6'11"   D. 7'1"

15. You are directed to pick up a tray load of brake shoes. The combined weight of tray and brake shoes is 4,000 pounds. Assume that each brake shoe weighs 40 pounds and the tray weighs 240 pounds.
The number of brake shoes in the tray is MOST NEARLY

15.____

    A. 88   B. 94   C. 100   D. 106

16. A maintainer earns $12.44 per hour, and time and one-half for overtime over 40 hours. Each week, 15 percent of his total salary is deducted for social security and taxes. Also, each week a $18.00 deduction is made for a savings bond and a $9.00 deduction is made for a charitable organization.
If he works a total of 46 hours in a week, his take-home pay for that week is

16.____

    A. $609.56   B. $518.10   C. $491.12   D. $410.70

17. A rectangularly-shaped repair facility for light trucks is 160 feet wide and 260 feet long. A 10-foot space is provided along each wall for benches and equipment. A 60-foot wide area in the middle of the floor is to remain clear for its entire 260 foot length. The entrance to the shop is at one end of this open area.
Assuming that there are no columns to contend with, the MAXIMUM area available for parking of trucks is _____ sq. ft.

17.____

    A. 15,600   B. 19,200   C. 26,000   D. 41,600

18. A criterion is established that limits the yearly major repair expenses to 30% of the current value of the equipment. Equipment is depreciated at a rate of 20% of its original cost each year. A truck purchased on January 1, 2000 for $9,000 had a reconditioned engine installed in February 2003 at a total cost of $900.
The amount of money available for additional major repairs on this truck in 2003 is

    A. none   B. $180   C. $360   D. $720

18.____

19. Twenty carburetors are ordered for your shop by the Purchasing Department. The terms are list, less 30% less 10%, less 5%.
If the list price of a carburetor is $70 and all terms are met upon delivery, the charges to your budget will be

    A. $1,359.60   B. $1,085.40   C. $837.90   D. $630.80

19.____

20. The sum of the fractions 7/16", 11/16", 5/32", and 7/8" is MOST NEARLY

    A. 2.1753"   B. 2.1563"   C. 1.9522"   D. 1.9463"

20.____

21. If 750 feet of wire weighs 60 lbs., the number of pounds that 150 feet will weigh is MOST NEARLY

    A. 12   B. 10   C. 8   D. 6

21.____

22. A steel rod 19.750" long is to have three pieces cut from its length. One piece is to be 3.250" long, the second 6.500" long, and the third piece 5.375".
If .125" is allowed for each cut, the length of the material left over is

    A. 3.750"   B. 4.250"   C. 4.500"   D. 5.150"

22.____

23. If the distance between the north and south terminals is 10.8 miles and a train makes six roundtrips, then the total travel mileage would be NEAREST _____ miles.

    A. 22   B. 65   C. 130   D. 145

23.____

24. If the thickness of material worn from a car wheel is approximately 1/16 inch off the diameter in 20,000 miles of travel, the wheel diameter will be reduced from 33 inches to 32 3/4 inches after _____ miles.

    A. 60,000   B. 80,000   C. 100,000   D. 120,000

24.____

25. If the distance between the north and south terminals is 11.3 miles and a train makes five roundtrips, then the total travel mileage would be NEAREST _____ miles.

    A. 23   B. 55   C. 115   D. 130

25.____

KEY (CORRECT ANSWERS)

1.	A	11.	B
2.	C	12.	A
3.	D	13.	D
4.	A	14.	B
5.	A	15.	B
6.	A	16.	C
7.	A	17.	B
8.	C	18.	B
9.	A	19.	C
10.	D	20.	B

21.	A
22.	B
23.	C
24.	B
25.	C

SOLUTIONS TO PROBLEMS

1. $\frac{3}{32}+\frac{3}{16}+\frac{3}{8}+\frac{3}{4}=\frac{45}{32}=1\frac{13}{32}$

2. Gross salary = ($11.52)(40) + ($17.28)(5) = $547.20

3. 2.620 ± .002 means from 2.618 to 2.622. The only selection in this range is 2.621.

4. ($60)($\frac{100}{50}$)+($25)($\frac{100}{25}$) $220 if made in the bus shop. Savings = $275 - $220 = $55

5. 9/16" + 11/32" + 15/64" + 1 3/32" =143/64 = 2 15/64" ≈ 2.234"

6. Diameter = 14.5" ÷ π ≈ 4.62"

7. ($20)($\frac{100}{50}$)+($10)($\frac{100}{25}$) = $80 if made in the bus shop. Savings = $90 - $80 = $10

8. [150 + [(30)(2 1/2)] - [(9)(5)] = [150+75] - 45 = 180, and 180/300 = 60%

9. (40)(60) ÷ 75 = 32

10. (1/4")(3/12) = 1/16" ≈ .062"

11. (20)(12) = 240", and 240" ÷ 9 1/2" ≈ 25.3, rounded down to 25 pieces of tubing

12. 14 3/8" - 7 5/8" - 5 1/4" - 1/16" = 1 3/8"

13. 12 7/16" + 14 5/16" + 9 3/16" + 9 1/8" + 6 1/4" + 5" = 56 5/16" ≈ 5 ft.

14. (2/3)(10') = 6 2/3' = 6'8"

15. 4000 - 240 = 3760 lbs. Then, 3760 ÷ 40 = 94 brake shoes

16. Take-home pay = ($12.44)(40)+($18.66)(6) - .15[($12.44)(40) + ($18.66)(6)] - $18.00 - $9.00 = $491.126 ≈ $491.12

17. Subtracting the area for benches and equipment would leave an area of 240' by 140'. Now, deduct the 60' width. Final area = (240')(80') = 19,200 sq.ft.

18. In 2003, the value of the truck = $9000 - (3)(.20)($9000) = $3600 The limit of the expenses for repairs = (.30)($3600) = $1080 After installing engine, $1080 - $900 = $180 left for additional major repairs.

19. (20)($70)(.70)(.90)(.95) = $837.90

20. 7/16" + 11/16" + 5/32" + 7/8" = 69/32" ≈ 2.1563"

21. (150/750)(60) = 12 lbs.

22. 19.750" - 3.250" - 6.500" - 5.375" - .125" - .125" - .125" = 4.250" left over

23. (6)(10.8)(2) = 129.6 ≈ 130 miles

24. 33" - 32 3/4" = 1/4". Then, (1/4 ÷ 1/16)(20,000) = 80,000 miles

25. (5)(11.3)(2) = 113 miles, closest to 115 miles

TEST 2

DIRECTIONS: Each question or incomplete statement is followed by several suggested answers or completions. Select the one that BEST answers the question or completes the statement. *PRINT THE LETTER OF THE CORRECT ANSWER IN THE SPACE AT THE RIGHT.*

1. In looking over an alteration job on car bodies, you find that 96 pieces of 1" x 1" x 1'6" long square steel stock are needed to do this job. Steel weighs 480 lbs. per cu. ft. and costs $0.12 per lb.
The total cost of this material is MOST NEARLY   1._____

   A. $40.00   B. $60.00   C. $80.00   D. $100.00

2. Assume that the breakdown cost of a particular motor job is as follows: 2._____
   Parts $160.00
   Labor   75.00
   Overhead   30.00
   The percentage of the total cost for labor is MOST NEARLY

   A.   20%   B.   25%   C.   28%   D.   32%

3. The engine hydraulic system and transmission on a certain type of tractor use the same type oil. This oil is delivered in 55 gallon drums.   3._____
   How many drums are needed to make all three changes on 10 of these tractors whose- capacities are the following:
   Engine   58 quarts
   Transmission   70 quarts
   Hydraulic system   22 gallons
   _____ drums.

   A.   100   B.   50   C.   54   D.   10

4. A new shop layout requires the following: 4._____
   1,000   sq.   ft.   for tool room
   3,000   sq.   ft.   for parts room
   10,000   sq.   ft.   for service bays
   5,500   sq.   ft.   for isles
   The building should be AT LEAST _____ yards wide and 70 yards long.

   A.   10   B.   20   C.   25   D.   30

5. When filling a diesel engine cooling system, the mix required is 80% antifreeze and 20% water. You are required to fill seven systems containing 30 gals. each. The number of 5 gallon cans of antifreeze that are required is MOST NEARLY   5._____

   A.   210   B.   168   C.   34   D.   26

6. The floors of 2 cars are to be painted with a special test paint. Assume that the floor area in each car is 600 square feet. A gallon of this paint will cover 400 square feet.   6._____
   The number of gallons of this paint that you should pick up at the storeroom to paint the two car floors would be

   A.   6   B.   5   C.   4   D.   3

7. Assume that you are sent to the storeroom for 1,000 of 600-volt contact tips which are to be distributed equally to 5 foremen, but you find that the storeroom can only supply you with 825.
If you distribute these 825 tips equally to the 5 foremen, the number of tips that each foreman will receive is

    A.   165   B.   175   C.   190   D.   200

7.____

8. You are asked to fill six 5-gallon cans of oil from a full drum containing 52 gallons.
When you have filled the six cans, the number of gallons of oil left in the drum will be MOST NEARLY

    A.   14   B.   16   C.   22   D.   30

8.____

9. A certain wire rope is made up of 6 strands, each strand containing 19 wires.
The TOTAL number of wires in this wire rope is

    A.   25   B.   96   C.   114   D.   144

9.____

10. The hook should be the weakest part of any crane, hoist, or sling.
According to this statement, if a particular hook has a rated capacity of 2 1/2 tons, then the MAXIMUM load that should be lifted with this hook is _____ pounds.

    A.   150   B.   3,000   C.   5,000   D.   5,500

10.____

11. Assume that 2 car wheels weigh 635 pounds each and are attached to an axle weighing 1,260 pounds.
The total weight of this assembly is MOST NEARLY _____ pounds.

    A.   1,270   B.   1,520   C.   1,895   D.   2,530

11.____

12. If an employee authorizes his employer to deduct 4% of his $300 weekly salary for a savings bond, the MINIMUM number of weekly deductions required to get enough money to buy a bond costing $36 is

    A.   3   B.   6   C.   8   D.   9

12.____

13. In weighing out a truckful of scrap metal, the scale reads 21,496 lbs.
If the empty truck weighs 9,879 lbs., the amount of scrap metal, in pounds, is MOST NEARLY

    A.   10,507   B.   10,602   C.   11,617   D.   12,617

13.____

14. Four trays of material are placed on the body of a delivery truck for delivery to the inspection shop. Each tray is 4 feet wide and 4 feet long.
If these trays are placed side by side on the floor of the delivery truck, together they will cover an area of the floor MOST NEARLY _____ square feet.

    A.   32   B.   48   C.   64   D.   72

14.____

15. Assume that you are operating a degreasing tank and its tray holds 5 gear cases. It takes 40 minutes to clean one tray of gear cases.
At the end of 6 hours of operation (excluding lunch break and loading and unloading time), the number of gear cases cleaned will be

    A.   30   B.   36   C.   45   D.   50

15.____

16. If a serviceman's weekly gross salary is $160 and 20% is deducted for taxes, his take-home pay is

    A. $120   B. $128   C. $140   D. $144

16._____

Questions 17-18.

DIRECTIONS: Questions 17 and 18 are to be answered on the basis of the following paragraph.

The car maintenance department is considering the purchase of a certain car part from Manufacturer X for $140. An equivalent part can be purchased from Manufacturer Y for $100. The part made by Manufacturer X must be reconditioned every 3 years, using material costing $30 and requiring 6 hours of labor. The part made by Manufacturer Y must be reconditioned every 1 1/2 years, using material costing $24 and requiring 5 hours of labor. The maintainer's rate of pay is $12 per hour.

17. The cost of operating with the part made by Manufacturer X (excluding the first cost) is MOST NEARLY _____ per year.

    A. $30   B. $32   C. $34   D. $42

17._____

18. The total cost of operating with the part made by Manufacturer Y over a period of 12 years, including the first cost of the part and assuming the part is scrapped at the end of 12 years, is MOST NEARLY

    A. $472   B. $572   C. $688   D. $772

18._____

19. The area of the steel plate shown in the sketch at the right is _____ sq. ft.

    A. 16
    B. 18
    C. 20
    D. 22

19._____

(Sketch dimensions: 4 FT, 1 FT, 2 FT, 4 FT, 7 FT)

20. A car part made by a Manufacturer X has a purchase cost of $7,500 and a life of 5 years. It requires a yearly maintenance cost of $50. Manufacturer Y offers a similar part of this type for $4,800, with a life of 3 years and a yearly maintenance cost of $75.
By purchasing the part offering a better overall value, the yearly savings per unit purchased would be

    A. $115   B. $125   C. $135   D. $140

20._____

21. A car part can be overhauled at the rate of 12 parts per hour. Each part requires new material costing $6 each. If the labor cost is $14 per hour, one part can be overhauled for a total cost (labor plus material) of MOST NEARLY

    A. $6.64   B. $7.16   C. $7.46   D. $8.20

21._____

22. A car part costs $150 per 50 units when purchased in a finished condition from a vendor. The car part can be made in the shop at a total cost of $2.20 per unit, when made on a machine which can be purchased for $1,000. The MINIMUM number of parts which must be made on this machine before the savings equal the cost of the machine is 22.____

    A.   850   B.   1,000   C.   1,250   D.   1,500

23. A pound of a certain type of metal washer contains 360 washers.
If 1/4 of the material of each washer is removed by enlarging the center of each washer, the number of washers to the pound should then be MOST NEARLY 23.____

    A.   280   B.   300   C.   380   D.   480

24. A maintainer earns $10.84 per hour, and time and one-half for overtime. Ten percent of his total salary earned is deducted from his paycheck for social security and taxes. He also contributes $5.00 per week to a charitable organization. No other deductions are made.
If he works 2 hours over his basic 40 hours, his weekly take-home pay should be MOST NEARLY 24.____

    A. $466.12   B. $419.50   C. $414.50   D. $410.60

25. A car part costs $130 per 100 units if purchased from a vendor. The car part can be made on a machine which can be purchased for $1,000. Assume that this machine has a production life of 20,000 units with no salvage value, and that all shop costs amount to $80 per 100 units turned out in the shop.
The money that would be SAVED during the life of the machine would be 25.____

    A. $800   B. $8,000   C. $9,000   D. $18,000

KEY (CORRECT ANSWERS)

1.	B	11.	D
2.	C	12.	A
3.	D	13.	C
4.	D	14.	C
5.	C	15.	C
6.	D	16.	B
7.	A	17.	C
8.	C	18.	C
9.	C	19.	C
10.	C	20.	B

21.	B
22.	C
23.	D
24.	C
25.	C

SOLUTIONS TO PROBLEMS

1. Total cost ≈ (96)(.01)(480)(.12) ≈ $55, which is closest to $60. Note that 1" x 1" x 1'6" ≈ (1/12')(1/12')(3/2')= 1/96 ≈ .01 cu. ft.

2. Labor = $75 ÷ $265 ≈ 28%

3. (10)(14.5+17.5+22) = 540. Then, 540 ÷ 55 ≈ 10 drums

4. Total sq.ft. = 19,500, which is 2166 2/3 sq.yds.

    Then, 2166 2/3 ÷ 70 ≈ 30.95 or 31

5. Amount of antifreeze = (.80)(7)(.30) = 168 gallons.

    Then, 2166 2/3 ÷ 70 ≈ 30.95 or 31

6. (600+600) ÷ 400 = 3 gallons

7. 825 ÷ 5 = 165 for each foreman

8. 52 - (6)(5) = 22 gallons left

9. (19)(6) = 114 wires

10. (2 1/2)(2000) = 5000 pounds

11. (2)(635) + 1260 = 2530 pounds

12. ($300)(.04) = $12. Then, $36 ÷ $12 = 3 weekly deductions

13. 21,496 - 9,879 = 11,617 pounds

14. 4(4')(4') = 64 sq.ft.

15. 6 hrs ÷ 2/3 hr. = 9 trays = 45 gear cases cleaned

16. Take-home pay = ($160)(.80) = $128

17. ($30) + (6)($12) = $102 for 3 yrs = $34 per year

18. 100 + 7(24) + 7(60) = 688

19. Separate the figure into regions as follows:

    I: 1'x2' = 2 sq.ft.

    II: 3'x4' = 12 sq.ft.

    III: (3'x4') ÷ 2' =6 sq.ft.

    Total = 20 sq.ft.

    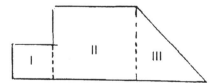

20. Manufacturer X: $7500 + ($50)(5) = $7750, so the cost per year is $7750 ÷ 5 = $1550.
    Manufacturer Y: $4800 + (3)($75) = $5025, so the cost per year is $5025 ÷ 3 = $1675
    Using Manufacturer X, savings = $125 per year

21. Cost of 12 parts = (12)($6) + $14 = $86. Then, cost of one part = $86 ÷ 12 ≈ $7.16

22. Savings per unit is &150/50 - $2.20 = $.80. Then, $1000 ÷ $.80 = 1250

23. 1 - 1/4 - 3/4. Then, 360 ÷ 3/4 = 480

24. Take-home pay = [($10.84)(40)+($16.26)(2)][.90] - $5 ≈ $414.50

25. Amount if purchased from a vendor = $130(200) = $26,000

    Using the machine, amount = $1000 + ($80)(200) = $17,000. Amount saved = $9000

TEST 3

DIRECTIONS: Each question or incomplete statement is followed by several suggested answers or completions. Select the one that BEST answers the question or completes the statement. *PRINT THE LETTER OF THE CORRECT ANSWER IN THE SPACE AT THE RIGHT.*

1. A Cat 983 Traxcavator can make a complete loading cycle from bank to truck and back to bank in 25 seconds.
   If the bucket contains 4 cu. yds. of loose material, the MINIMUM amount of material that an operator should load in 4 hours is _____ cubic yards.

   A. 2,304   B. 2,100   C. 1,896   D. 576

   1.____

2. An excavation is 12' x 18' x 15' and is to be dug by a Cat 983 Traxcavator with 3 cubic yards of solid material excavated per pass.
   The MINIMUM number of passes required to dig the hole is _____ passes.

   A. 40   B. 46   C. 120   D. 126

   2.____

3. A Cat D8 tractor and 463 scraper can haul 22 cubic yards of cover material per trip.
   If it is required to cover an area 1,000 feet by 100 feet to a depth of 2 feet, the MINI-MUM number of trips that will be required is MOST NEARLY

   A. 284   B. 337   C. 385   D. 421

   3.____

4. Gravel weighs 2,800 pounds per cubic yard.
   In order to carry 42,000 pounds of gravel, the capacity of a truck must be AT LEAST _____ cubic yards.

   A. 10   B. 12   C. 15   D. 18

   4.____

5. The average capacity of an Athey Wagon is 60 cubic yards. The Cat D8 tractor pulls 2 wagons.
   The MINIMUM number of trips to the fill that would be required to empty a barge loaded with 1,000 cubic yards of refuse is

   A. 9   B. 17   C. 30   D. 90

   5.____

6. When pulling 2 Athey trailers, the operator of a Cat D8 tractor can make a roundtrip from the crane to the fill and back in 15 minutes.
   Assuming that delays and breaks allow the man to work productively for 75% of the shift, the MAXIMUM number of trips that the operator can make in an 8-hour shift is

   A. 43   B. 32   C. 24   D. 16

   6.____

7. In plowing a street which is 24 feet wide, a motor grader can make an 8-ft. wide pass, with a 2-ft. overlap.
   If a roundtrip takes 4 minutes, the MINIMUM time needed to plow this street should be _____ minutes.

   A. 12   B. 16   C. 24   D. 32

   7.____

8. A scraper is loaded with 23 cubic yards of sand weighing 100 pounds per cubic foot.
   The weight of the load, in tons, is MOST NEARLY

   A. 20   B. 30   C. 40   D. 60

   8.____

9. Assume a crankcase oil change of 6 quarts for every 150 service hours. 9.____
   How many 42 gallon drums of oil are required for 8,400 total service hours?

   A.   5   B.   2   C.   1   D.   1 1/3

10. Assume that a ruler is marked in 10ths of a foot instead of in inches. 10.____
    5 tenths on this ruler would be

    A.   4"   B.   5"   C.   6"   D.   7"

11. A truck load of 1 1/2" stone from a 10 cubic yard truck will spread an area APPROXI- 11.____
    MATELY _____ long, 6" deep, and _____ wide.

    A.   50'; 10'   B.   10'; 5'   C.   54'; 10'   D.   45'; 5'

12. A dump truck with a body 10 ft. long, 5 ft. wide, and 4 ft. deep has a volume of _____ 12.____
    cubic feet.

    A.   150   B.   200   C.   250   D.   300

13. A tractor is operated on a given landfill operation during the following time intervals in one 13.____
    day: from 8:15 A.M. to 11:45 A.M.; from 12:30 P.M. to 6:00 P.M.; from 6:45 P.M. to 11:30
    P.M.
    The total net operating time, expressed in hours and minutes, is MOST NEARLY
    _____ hours, _____ minutes.

    A.   13; 30   B.   13; 15   C.   13; 45   D.   12; 45

14. The area of ground contact (with standard track shoes) of a late model D8 Caterpillar 14.____
    Tractor is 4,296 sq. in. Expressed in square feet, this is MOST NEARLY

    A.   358   B.   29.8   C.   159.3   D.   21.37

15. A towing winch develops a bare drum line pull of 11.8 tons. 15.____
    This force represents, in pounds,

    A.   23,850   B.   28,300   C.   23,800   D.   23,600

16. The fuel tank gauge reads about 3/4 of a full tank. 16.____
    If the tank capacity is 72.5 gallons, the amount of fuel in the tank is MOST NEARLY

    A.   53.2   B.   53.8   C.   54.5   D.   55.0

17. If a dump truck capable of carrying 40 2/3 cubic yards is 3/4 loaded, it is carrying, in 17.____
    cubic yards,

    A.   28   B.   36 1/2   C.   30 1/2   D.   28 2/3

18. A load of sand filling a truck body 6 feet long, 5 feet wide, and 3 feet deep would contain 18.____
    _____ cubic feet.

    A.   14   B.   90   C.   33   D.   21

Questions 19-21.

DIRECTIONS: Questions 19 through 21 are to be answered on the basis of the diagrams of balanced levers shown below. P is the center of rotation, W is the weight on the lever, and F is the balancing force.

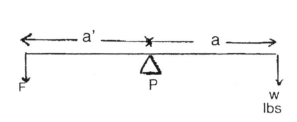 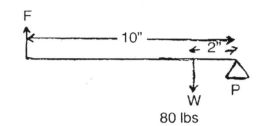

19. In Diagram 1, the force F required to balance the weight W lbs. on the lever shown is equal to _____ lbs.

   A. a/W   B. W/a   C. W   D. Wa   19._____

20. In Diagram 2, the force F required to balance the weight of 80 lbs. on the lever shown is _____ lbs.

   A. 4   B. 3   C. 16   D. 32   20._____

21. The mechanical advantage of the lever shown in Diagram 2 is

   A. 4   B. 5   C. 8   D. 12   21._____

22. The specific gravity of a liquid may be defined as the ratio of the weight of a given volume of the liquid to the weight of an equal volume of water. An empty bottle weighs 5 oz. When the bottle is filled with water, the total weight is 50 oz. When the bottle is filled with another liquid, the total weight is 95 oz.
   The specific gravity of the second liquid is MOST NEARLY   22._____

   A. .50   B. .58   C. 1.7   D. 2.0

23. If one inch is approximately equal to 2.54 centimeters, the number of inches in one meter is MOST NEARLY   23._____

   A. 14.2   B. 25.4   C. 39.4   D. 91.4

24. One-quarter divided by five-eighths is   24._____

   A. 5/32   B. 1/10   C. 2/5   D. 5/2

25. A man works on a certain job continuously, with no time off for lunch.   25._____
   If he works from 9:45 A.M. until 1:35 P.M. to finish the job, the total time which he spent on the job is MOST NEARLY _____ hours, _____ minutes.

   A. 3; 10   B. 3; 35   C. 3; 50   D. 4; 15

KEY (CORRECT ANSWERS)

1.	A		11.	C
2.	A		12.	B
3.	B		13.	C
4.	C		14.	B
5.	A		15.	D
6.	C		16.	C
7.	B		17.	C
8.	B		18.	B
9.	B		19.	C
10.	C		20.	C

21.	B
22.	D
23.	C
24.	C
25.	C

———

SOLUTIONS TO PROBLEMS

1. 4 hrs = (4)(60)(60) = 14,400 sec. Then, 14,400 ÷ 25 = 576 Thus, (576)(4 cu.yds.) = 2304 cu.yds.

2. (12')(18')(15') = 3240 cu.ft. = 120 cu.yds. Then, 120 ÷ 3 = 40

3. (1000')(100')(2') = 200,000 cu.ft. ≈ 7407.4 cu.yds.
   Finally, 7407.4 ÷ 22 = 336.7, rounded up to 337 trips.

4. 42,000 ÷ 2800 = 15 cu.yds.

5. (2)(60 cu.yds.) = 120 yds. Then, 1000 ÷ 120 = 8 1/3, which must be rounded up to 9 trips

6. 8 hrs ÷ 15 min = 32. Then, (32)(.75) = 24 trips

7. 24' ÷ 8' = 3; however, with a 2 ft. overlap, only 6' gets plowed. So, (24 ÷ 6)(4 min) = 16 min.

8. 23 cu.yds. = 621 cu.ft. Then, (621)(100) = 62,100 lbs.
   Finally, 62,100 ÷ 2000 ≈ 30 tons

9. 8400 ÷ 150 = 56. Then, (56)(6 qts) = 336 qts = 84 gallons
   Finally, 84 ÷ 42 = 2 drums

10. 5 tenths = (5/10)(12") = 6"

11. (54')(1/2')(10') = 270 cu.ft. = 10 cu.yds.

12. Volume = (10')(5')(4') = 200 cu.ft.

13. 3 hrs. 30 min. + 5 hrs. 30 min. + 4 hrs. 45 min. = 12 hrs. 105 min. = 13 hrs. 45 min.

14. 4296 sq.in. = 4296 ÷ 144 ≈ 29.8 sq.ft.

15. 11.8 tons = (11.8)(2000) = 23,600 lbs.

16. (72.5)(.75) = 54.375, closest to 54.5 gallons

17. (40 2/3)(3/4) = 30 1/2 cu.yds.

18. (6')(5')(3') = 90 cu.ft.

19. F = Wa/a = W lbs.

20. F = (80)(2) ÷ 10 = 16 lbs.

21. Mechanical advantage = 10/2 = 5

22. Specific gravity = $\dfrac{95-5}{50-5} = 2$

23. 1 meter = 100 cm. ≈ (100) ÷ (2.54) ≈ 39.4 in.

24. $1/4 ÷ 5/8 = \dfrac{1}{4} \cdot \dfrac{8}{5} = \dfrac{2}{5}$

25. 9:45 AM to 1:35 PM = 3 hrs. 50 min.

INTERPRETING STATISTICAL DATA
GRAPHS, CHARTS AND TABLES

EXAMINATION SECTION
TEST 1

DIRECTIONS: Each question or incomplete statement is followed by several suggested answers or completions. Select the one that BEST answers the question or completes the statement. *PRINT THE LETTER OF THE CORRECT ANSWER IN THE SPACE AT THE RIGHT.*

Questions 1-3.

DIRECTIONS: Questions 1 through 3 are to be answered on the basis of the following charts and information.

AREA 1

Section A	Section B
Stationery	Electrical supplies
Office supplies	Lighting equipment
Kitchenware	Dry goods

AREA 2

Section A	Section B
Drugs	Tools
Chemicals	Laboratory equipment
Cleaning supplies	Hospital supplies

The above charts represent a storage room which is separated into two areas, Area 1 and Area 2, and separated within each area into two sections, Section A and Section B. Each section stores the items shown on the charts.

1. According to the above charts, you should find laboratory equipment in Area _____, Section _____.

    A. 1; A   B. 1; B   C. 2; A   D. 2; B

1.____

2. According to the above charts, all of the following items are in Area 1, Section A EXCEPT

    A. dry goods   B. stationery
    C. kitchenware   D. office supplies

2.____

3. According to the above charts, you should store light bulbs in Area _____, Section _____.

    A. 1; A   B. 1; B   C. 2; A   D. 2; B

3.____

KEY (CORRECT ANSWERS)

1. D
2. A
3. B

———

TEST 2

Questions 1-3.

DIRECTIONS: Questions 1 through 3 are to be answered on the basis of the information given in the stock listing below.

STOCK LISTING OF BOLTS, NUTS, SCREWS, WASHERS, ETC.

Item No.	Commodity Code	Description
1	43-A00059	Anchor Expansion Mach Screw Type 6/32 inch
2	43-A00061	Anchor Expansion Mach Screw Type 8/32 inch
3	43-B06028	Bolt Carriage Oval HD Hex Nut 3/16 x 1 inch
4	43-B06029	Bolt Carriage Oval HD Hex Nut 3/16 x 1 1/2 inch
5	43-N06033	Nut Mach Screw Brass Hex 4/40 inch
6	43-N04725	Nut Mach Screw Brass Hex 6/40 inch
7	43-S08963	Screw Mach Brass Rnd HD 6/32 x 1 inch
8	43-S08975	Screw Mach Brass Rnd HD 6/32 x 2 inch
9	43-W00700	Washer Brass Round 1 lb. pkg No. 4
10	43-W03024	Washer Brass Round 1 lb. pkg No. 6

1.   The type of item which is described as 1 lb. pkg is a   1.____

   A.   bolt   B.   nut   C.   screw   D.   washer

2.   The Commodity Code which appears in the next row below Commodity Code 43-B06029   2.____
   is

   A.   43-A00061   B.   43-B06028   C.   43-N06033   D.   43-N04725

3.   The one of the following which does NOT have the complete information taken from the   3.____
   Description column of the item is

   A.   Anchor Expansion Mach Screw Type 8/32 inch
   B.   Bolt Carriage Oval Nut 3/16 x 1 1/2 inch
   C.   Nut Mach Screw Brass Hex 6/40 inch
   D.   Screw Mach Brass Rnd HD 6/32 x 2 inch

KEY (CORRECT ANSWERS)

1.   D
2.   C
3.   B

TEST 3

Questions 1-3.

DIRECTIONS: Questions 1 through 3 are to be answered on the basis of the information given in the chart shown below.

Item	Weight
Metal file box	5 pounds
Large desk stapler	2 pounds
Large tape dispenser	1.5 pounds
Hardcover dictionary	3 pounds

1. Based on the figures shown in the chart above, the TOTAL weight of 5 metal file boxes, 3 hardcover dictionaries, and a large tape dispenser is _____ pounds.   1.____

   A. 33.5   B. 34.5   C. 35.5   D. 36.5

2. Of the following, which group of items would weigh a TOTAL of 25 pounds or less?   2.____

   A. 6 metal file boxes and 1 hardcover dictionary
   B. 10 large desk staplers and 1 hardcover dictionary
   C. 8 hardcover dictionaries and 2 large tape dispensers
   D. 10 large tape dispensers and 3 metal file boxes

3. Assume that 5 large desk staplers, 6 metal file boxes, 10 hardcover dictionaries, and 3 large tape dispensers are placed in a shipping container with a weight limit of 100 pounds.   3.____
   When you add up the total weight of the items, the number of pounds under the weight limit would be _____ pounds.

   A. 23.5   B. 24.5   C. 25.5   D. 26.5

_____

KEY (CORRECT ANSWERS)

1. C
2. B
3. C

_____

TEST 4

Questions 1-5.

DIRECTIONS: Questions 1 through 5 are to be answered on the basis of the information given in the stock listing below.

LISTING OF ENVELOPES IN STOCK

Item No.	Description	Unit of Issue (per carton)	Amount (cartons)
1	Envelope Commercial White 3 5/8" x 6 1/2"	1000	14
2	Envelope Commercial White 4 1/2" x 9 1/2"	2500	7
3	Envelope Open End Metal Clasp 7" x 10"	1000	16
4	Envelope Open End Metal Clasp 8 1/2" x 11 1/2"	1000	15
5	Envelope Open End Metal Clasp 9 1/2" x 12 1/2"	500	28
6	Envelope Open End Metal Clasp 11 1/2" x 14 1/2"	500	24

1. The TOTAL number of cartons of envelopes in stock is   1._____

   A. 87   B. 84   C. 100   D. 104

2. The envelopes which all have a unit of issue of 1000 per carton are found in Item Nos.   2._____

   A. 1, 2, and 3   B. 1, 3, and 4
   C. 2, 4, and 5   D. 3, 4, and 6

3. The item for which there is the GREATEST number of envelopes in stock is Item No.   3._____

   A. 2   B. 3   C. 4   D. 5

4. The TOTAL number of envelopes in stock for all of the items listed above is   4._____

   A. 74,000   B. 81,000   C. 88,500   D. 104,500

5. You receive an order for the following items: Item No. 1, 2000 envelopes; Item No. 2, 5000 envelopes; Item No. 4, 2000 envelopes; Item No. 6, 1000 envelopes.   5._____
   The TOTAL number of cartons that you will have to pick from stock in filling the order is

   A. 6   B. 7   C. 8   D. 9

KEY (CORRECT ANSWERS)

1. D
2. B
3. A
4. C
5. C

TEST 5

DIRECTIONS: Each question or incomplete statement is followed by several suggested answers or completions. Select the one that BEST answers the question or completes the statement. *PRINT THE LETTER OF THE CORRECT ANSWER IN THE SPACE AT THE RIGHT.*

Questions 1-5.

DIRECTIONS: Questions 1 through 5 are to be answered on the basis of the information given in Tables 1 and 2 of the DAILY PRODUCTIVITY REPORT shown below.

DAILY PRODUCTIVITY REPORT

Table 1

Standards	Unsatisfactory	Conditional	Satisfactory	Superior	Outstanding
Number of pieces packed per day	245 and below	246 to 289	290 to 347	348 to 405	406 and above

Table 2

Initials of the packer	A.S.	S.B.	B.D.	L.M.	J.C.	R.N.	B.G.	C.A.	D.F.	E.R.
Number of Pieces Packed Per Day	252	335	276	342	409	290	235	309	246	425

1. The number of packers whose productivity is *Outstanding* is   1.____

   A. 4   B. 3   C. 2   D. 1

2. The number of packers who come under the *Conditional* productivity standard is   2.____

   A. 1   B. 2   C. 3   D. 4

3. The percentage of packers whose productivity can be rated *Satisfactory* or higher is   3.____

   A. 30%   B. 40%   C. 50%   D. 60%

4. If every packer's daily productivity increased by 20 pieces, the number of packers whose productivity ratings would change to the NEXT standard is   4.____

   A. 4   B. 5   C. 6   D. 7

5. Which one of the following is an ACCURATE statement that can be made based on the   5.____
    information shown in Tables 1 and 2?

    A. There are more packers whose productivity is above the maximum Satisfactory
        level than below the minimum Satisfactory level.
    B. There are more packers whose productivity is in the Satisfactory standard than in
        any one of the other four standards.
    C. The number of packers whose productivity is Unsatisfactory is equal to the number
        of packers whose productivity is Outstanding.
    D. There is at least one packer whose productivity is in each of the five standards.

KEY (CORRECT ANSWERS)

1. C
2. C
3. D
4. A
5. B

TEST 6

Questions 1-4.

DIRECTIONS: Questions 1 through 4 are to be answered on the basis of the information given in the inventory tables shown below. Table 1 shows the amount of each item in stock according to the information contained on the perpetual inventory card for that item. Table 2 shows the amount of the same item in stock according to an inventory just completed by the staff.

Table 1

Perpetual Inventory Card	
Item No.	Amount of Stock
A107	2,564
A257	10,365
A342	7,018
A475	52,475
B026	16,207
B422	4,520
B717	21,431
B802	308
C328	594
C329	164
C438	723
C527	844

Table 2

Inventory Just Completed By Staff	
Item No.	Amount of Stock
A107	2,545
A257	10,356
A342	7,018
A475	52,475
B026	16,207
B422	4,505
B717	21,413
B802	308
C328	594
C329	143
C438	723
C527	854

1. In which one of the following items is there a difference between the amount of stock shown on the perpetual inventory card and in the inventory just completed? Item No.

   A. A257   B. B026   C. C328   D. C438

2. In which one of the following items is the difference GREATEST between the amount of stock shown on the perpetual inventory card and in the inventory just completed? Item No.

   A. A107   B. B422   C. B717   D. C329

3. The amount of stock shown for Item No. C527 on the inventory taken by the staff is greater than the amount shown on the perpetual inventory card.
   Of the following, the LEAST likely reason for this difference is that the

   A. perpetual inventory card was not brought up to date
   B. staff did not take an accurate inventory
   C. information entered on the perpetual inventory card was inaccurate
   D. staff made an inventory on the wrong item

4. Which one of the following is an ACCURATE statement that can be made based on the information shown in Tables 1 and 2?

   A. More than half of the items listed show a difference between the amount of stock shown on the perpetual inventory card and in the inventory just completed.
   B. One-third of the items listed show the amount of stock on the perpetual inventory card and in the inventory just completed to be 10,000 or more.

C. Less than half of the items listed show a difference between the amount of stock shown on the perpetual inventory card and in the inventory just completed.
D. One-third of the items listed show the amount of stock on the perpetual inventory card and in the inventory just completed to be 10,000 or less.

———

KEY (CORRECT ANSWERS)

1. A
2. D
3. D
4. B

———

TEST 7

Questions 1-3.

DIRECTIONS: Questions 1 through 3 are to be answered on the basis of the information given in the chart below.

ITEM NUMBER TOTALS AS OF JANUARY 31, 2009

Item No.	Monthly Usage	Current Inventory	Time Required Between Ordering & Delivery of Item
1	460	1,000	1 month
2	475	1,500	2 months
3	225	1,500	4 months
4	500	2,500	5 months
5	1,150	1,950	2 months
6	775	4,700	5 months
7	850	1,700	2 months
8	900	3,600	3 months
9	175	525	2 months
10	1,325	5,300	3 months
11	225	900	4 months
12	425	1,500	1 month

1. Which one of the following, if not ordered by February 1, 2009, would cause the monthly usage to exceed the current inventory before new merchandise could be received?
   Item No.

   A. 1   B. 4   C. 6   D. 10

   1._____

2. Which one of the following must be ordered immediately because the current inventory cannot cover the monthly usage?
   Item No.

   A. 2   B. 3   C. 5   D. 12

   2._____

3. The date by which Item Numbers 8, 9, and 10 must be ordered so that the monthly usage does NOT exceed the current inventory is _____, 2009.

   A. February 1   B. March 1
   C. April 1   D. May 1

   3._____

KEY (CORRECT ANSWERS)

1. B
2. C
3. B

REPORT WRITING

EXAMINATION SECTION
TEST 1

DIRECTIONS: Each question or incomplete statement is followed by several suggested answers or completions. Select the one that BEST answers the question or completes the statement. *PRINT THE LETTER OF THE CORRECT ANSWER IN THE SPACE AT THE RIGHT.*

Questions 1-5.

DIRECTIONS: Questions 1 through 5 are to be answered SOLELY on the basis of the following report.

REPORT OF DEFECTIVE EQUIPMENT

DEPARTMENT:*Social Services*   REPORT NO.*3026*
DIVISION: *Personnel*   DATE OF REPORT;*5/27*
ROOM: *120B*

DEFECTIVE EQUIPMENT:*Six office telephones with pick-up and hold buttons*

NUMBERS OF DEFECTIVE TELEPHONES: *525-0102, 3, 4, and 5*

DESCRIPTION OF DEFECT: *Marjorie Black, a Clerk, called on 5/22 to report that the button lights for the four lines on all six telephones in her office were not functioning and it was, therefore, impossible to know which lines were in use. On 5/26,, Howard Perl, Admin. Asst., called in regard to the same telephones. He was annoyed because no repairs had been made and stated that all the employees in his unit were being inconvenienced. He requested prompt repair service.*

Ruth Gomez
SIGNATURE OF REPORTING EMPLOYEE
Sr. Telephone Operator

TITLE

JUDITH O'LAUGHLIN
SIGNATURE OF SUPERVISOR

TO BE COMPLETED
AFTER SERVICING
DATE: *5/28*
APPROVED: *Judy O'Laughlin*

1. The person who made a written report about the improper functioning of telephones in the Personnel division is   1.____

    A. Marjorie Black   B. Ru'th Gomez
    C. Howard Perl   D. Judith O'Laughlin

2. How many days elapsed between the original request for telephone repair service and the completion of service?   2.____

    A. 2   B. 4   C. 5   D. 6

3. Of the following, the only information NOT given in the report is   3.____

    A. number of employees affected by the defective service
    B. number of the report
    C. number of telephones with a button defect
    D. telephone numbers of the defective phones

4. The one of the following items of information which would have been LEAST helpful to the repairman who was assigned this repair job is that   4.____

    A. the defect involved pick-up buttons for 4 serviced lines
    B. the location is Room 120B in the Department of Social Services
    C. Marjorie Black initially reported the defective equipment
    D. six telephone units need to be repaired

5. Which of the following statements is CORRECT concerning the people mentioned in the report?   5.____

    A. Ruth Gomez has a higher title than Judith O'Laughlin.
    B. Judith O'Laughlin's signature appears twice on this form.
    C. Howard Perl reported on May 25 that the telephones needed adjusting.
    D. Marjorie Black reported that she was disturbed that no repairs had been made.

Questions 6-10.

DIRECTIONS: Questions 6 through 10 are based on the UNUSUAL OCCURRENCE REPORT given below. Five phrases in the report have been removed and are listed below the report as 1. through 5. In each of the five places where phrases of the report have been left out, the number of a question has been inserted. For each question, select the number of the missing phrase which would make the report read correctly.

UNUSUAL OCCURRENCE REPORT

POST _____
TOUR _____
DATE _____

Location of Occurrence: _____

REMARKS: While making rounds this morning, I thought that I heard some strange sounds coming from Storeroom #55. Upon investigation, I saw that _6_ and that the door to the storeroom was slightly opened. At 2:45 A.M., I _7_.

Suddenly two men jumped out from _8_, dropped the tools which they were holding, and made a dash for the door. I ordered them to stop, but they just kept running.

I was able to get a good look at both of them. One man was wearing a green jacket and had a full beard, and the other was short and had blond hair. Immediately, I called the police; and about two minutes later, I notified 9 . I 10 the police arrived, and I gave them the complete details of the incident.

<u>Security Officer Donald Rimson 23807</u>
Signature　　　　Pass No.

1. the special inspection control desk
2. behind some crates
3. the lock had been tampered with
4. remained at the storeroom until
5. entered the storeroom and began to look around

6.　A. 1　　　　B. 3　　　　C. 4　　　　D. 5　　　　6._____

7.　A. 2　　　　B. 3　　　　C. 4　　　　D. 5　　　　7._____

8.　A. 1　　　　B. 2　　　　C. 3　　　　D. 4　　　　8._____

9.　A. 1　　　　B. 2　　　　C. 3　　　　D. 4　　　　9._____

10.　A. 2　　　　B. 3　　　　C. 4　　　　D. 5　　　　10._____

Questions 11-13.

DIRECTIONS: Below is a report consisting of 15 numbered sentences, some of which are not consistent with the principles of good report writing. Questions 11 through 13 are to be answered SOLELY on the basis of the information contained in the report and your knowledge of investigative principles and practices.

To:　　Tom Smith, Administrative Investigator
From:　John Jones, Supervising Investigator

1. On January 7, I received a call from Mrs. H. Harris of 684 Sunset Street, Brooklyn.
2. Mrs. Harris informed me that she wanted to report an instance of fraud relating to public assistance payments being received by her neighbor, Mrs. I Wallace.
3. I advised her that such a subject would best be discussed in person.
4. I then arranged a field visitation for January 10 at Mrs. Harris' apartment, 684 Sunset Street, Brooklyn.
5. On January 10, I discussed the basis for Mrs. Harris' charge against Mrs. Wallace at the former's apartment.
6. She stated that her neighbor is receiving Aid to Dependent Children payments for seven children, but that only three of her children are still living with her.
7. In addition, Mrs. Harris also claimed that her husband, whom she reported to the authorities as missing, usually sees her several times a week.
8. After further questioning, Mrs. Harris admitted to me that she had been quite friendly with Mrs. Wallace until they recently argued about trash left in their adjoining hall corridor.
9. However, she firmly stated that her allegations against Mrs. Wallace were valid and that she feared repercussions for her actions.
10. At the completion of the interview, I assured Mrs. Harris of the confidentiality of her statements and that an attempt would be made to verify her allegations.

11. As I was leaving Mrs. Harris' apartment, I noticed a man, aged approximately 45, walking out of Mrs. Wallace's apartment.
12. I followed him until he entered a late model green Oldsmobile and sped away.
13. On January 3, I returned to 684 Sunset Court, having determined that Mrs. Wallace is receiving assistance as indicated by Mrs. Harris.
14. However, upon presentation of official identification Mrs. Wallace refused to admit me to her apartment or grant an interview.
15. I am therefore referring this matter to you for further instructions.

John Jones
Supervising Investigator

11. The one of the following statements that clearly lacks vital information is Statement   11.____

    A. 8   B. 10   C. 12   D. 14

12. Which of the following sentences from the report is ambiguous?   12.____
Sentence

    A. 2   B. 3   C. 7   D. 10

13. Which of the following sentences contains information contradicting other data in the   13.____
above report? Sentence

    A. 3   B. 8   C. 10   D. 13

Questions 14-16.

DIRECTIONS: Questions 14 through 16 are to be answered on the basis of the following report.

To: Ralph King   Date: April 3
        Senior Menagerie Keeper

                                    Subject:

From: William Rattner
        Menagerie Keeper

This memorandum is to inform you of the disappearance of the boa constrictor from the Reptile Collection in the Main Building.

This morning upon entering the room, I realized that the snake was missing. After having asked around, I am of the opinion that the boa constrictor has been stolen. Since there are no signs of forced entry, it seems likely that whoever removed the snake from the premises entered the room through a window which had been left unlocked the previous night. I, therefore, suggest that all zoo personnel be more concerned with proper security measures in the future so that something like this does not happen again.

14. Which one of the following pieces of information has been OMITTED from the report by the Menagerie Keeper?   14.____

    A. Action taken by him after his discovery that the boa constrictor was missing
    B. The date that the disappearance of the boa constrictor was noted
    C. The time that the disappearance of the boa constrictor was noted
    D. The building in which the boa constrictor was kept

15. Based upon information contained in the above paragraph, which of the following statements would be BEST as the subject of this report?   15.____

    A. Request for more effective security measures in the zoo
    B. Vandalism in the zoo
    C. Disappearance of boa constrictor
    D. Request for replacement of boa constrictor

16. According to the above report, which of the following statements CANNOT be considered factual?   16.____

    A. The boa constrictor was being kept in the Main Building.
    B. The boa constrictor is missing.
    C. All zoo personnel are careless about security measures.
    D. There are no signs of forced entry.

Questions 17-19.

DIRECTIONS: Questions 17 through 19 are to be answered on the basis of the Accident Report below. Read this report carefully before answering the questions. Select your answers ONLY on the basis of this report.

ACCIDENT REPORT
Feb. 14

    On February 14 at 3:45 P.M., Mr. Warren, while on the top of a stairway at the 34th Street Station, realized the *D* train was in the station loading passengers. In his haste to catch the train, he forcefully ran down the stairs, pushing aside three other people also going down the stairs. Mr. Parker, one of the three people, lost his footing and fell to the bottom of the stairs. Working on the platform, I saw Mr. Parker lose his footing as a result of Mr. Warren's actions, and I immediately went to his aid. Assistant Station Supervisor Brown was attracted to the incident after a crowd had gathered. After 15 minutes, the injured man, Mr. Parker, got up and boarded a train that was in the station and, therefore, he was not hurt seriously.

                                         R. Sands #3214
                                         Conductor

17. Since accident reports should only contain facts, which of the following should NOT be put into the accident report?   17.____

    A. The incident took place at the 34th Street Station.
    B. Mr. Parker was not hurt seriously.
    C. The date that the report was written
    D. Mr. Sands went to the aid of the injured man

18. The title of the person submitting the report was   18.____

    A.   Porter
    B.   Assistant Station Supervisor
    C.   Conductor
    D.   Passenger

19. The TOTAL number of different persons mentioned in this report is   19.____

    A. seven   B. six   C. five   D. four

Questions 20-24.

DIRECTIONS: Questions 20 through 24 are to be answered SOLELY on the basis of the following report which is similar to those used in departments for reporting accidents.

REPORT OF ACCIDENT

Date of Accident: 3/21   Time: 3:43 P.M.   Date of Report: 3/24

Department Vehicle
Operator's Name: James Doe Title: Motor Vehicle Operator
Vehicle Code No.: 22-187
License Plate No.: 3N-1234

Damage to Vehicle: Right rear fender ripped, hubcap dented, rear bumper twisted

Place of Accident: 8th Avenue & 48th Street

Vehicle No. 2
Operator's Name: Richard Roe
Operator's Address: 841 W. 68th St.
Owner's Name: Jane Roe
Owner's Address: 2792 Beal Ave.
License Plate No.: 8Y-6789

Damage to Vehicle: Grill, radiator, right side of front bumper, rightfront fender and headlight crushed

Description of Accident: I was driving east on 48th Street with the green light. I was almost across 8th Avenue when Ford panel truck started north and crashed into my rear right fender. Driver of Ford used abussive language and accused me of rolling into his truck.

Persons Injured

Name <u>Richard Roe</u>   Address <u>841 W. 68th Street</u>
Name _____   Address _____
Name _____   Address _____

Witnesses

Name Richard Roe   Address 841 W. 68th Street
Name John Brown   Address 226 South Avenue
Name Mary Green   Address 42 East Street

Report Prepared By James Doe
Title MVO   Badge No. 11346

20. According to the above description of the accident, the diagram that would BEST show   20._____
how and where the vehicles crashed is

21. Of the following words used in the report, the one spelled INCORRECTLY is   21._____

    A. abussive   B. accused   C. radiator   D. twisted

22. The city vehicle involved in this accident can BEST be identified   22._____

    A. as a panel truck
    B. the Department vehicle
    C. by the Badge Number of the operator
    D. by the Vehicle Code Number

23. According to the information in the report, the right-of-way belonged to   23.____

    A.   neither vehicle   B.   the Department vehicle
    C.   the vehicle that took it   D.   Vehicle No. 2

24. An entry on the report that seems to be INCORRECT is the   24.____

    A.   first witness   B.   second witness
    C.   third witness   D.   owner's name

25. Assume that the following passage is taken from a report which you, a deputy chief,   25.____
receive from a battalion chief under your command. The report relates to a fire for which
the department received public criticism because of delay in response and extension of
fire to neighboring buildings.
Alarm from box _____ was received at 5:13 P.M. on Friday,
October 2. All first alarm companies departed from quarters expeditiously but progress
along the vehicle-glutted arterial thoroughfares was agonizingly slow. By dint of
extraordinary effort and by virtue of great skill in maneuvering through impassable traf-
fic, Engine Co._____ arrived at the scene at 5:21 P.M. The sight which greeted them
was a virtual Dante 's INFERNO, of holocaust proportions. The hub of the conflagra-
tion was the penultimate structure of a row of houses, with extension impending to
contiguous edifices...
The MAIN fault with the above report is that it

    A.   contains spelling and punctuation errors
    B.   contains unnecessary details
    C.   uses words not in accordance with dictionary definitions
    D.   uses inappropriate language and style

KEY (CORRECT ANSWERS)

1.	B		11.	C
2.	D		12.	C
3.	A		13.	D
4.	C		14.	C
5.	B		15.	C
6.	B		16.	C
7.	D		17.	B
8.	B		18.	C
9.	A		19.	B
10.	C		20.	A

21.	A
22.	D
23.	B
24.	A
25.	D

TEST 2

DIRECTIONS: Each question or incomplete statement is followed by several suggested answers or completions. Select the one that BEST answers the question or completes the statement. *PRINT THE LETTER OF THE CORRECT ANSWER IN THE SPACE AT THE RIGHT.*

Questions 1-4.

DIRECTIONS: Questions 1 through 4 are to be answered on the basis of the information in the report below.

To: Chief, Division X From:
            Mrs. Helen Jones, Clerk
Subject: Accident involving two employees, Mr. John Smith and Mr. Robert Brown

On February 15, Mr. Smith and Mr. Brown were injured in an accident occurring in the shop at 10 Long Road. No one was in the area of the accident other than Mr. Smith and Mr. Brown. Both of these employees described the following circumstances:

1. Mr. Brown saw the largest tool on the wall begin to fall from where it was hanging and ran up to push Mr. Smith out of the way and to prevent the tool from falling, if possible.
2. Mr. Smith was standing near the wall under some tools which were hanging on nails in the wall.
3. Mr. Brown was standing a few steps from the wall.
4. Mr. Brown stepped toward Mr. Smith, who was on the floor and away from the falling tool. He tripped and fell over a piece of equipment on the floor.
5. Mr. Brown pushed Mr. Smith, who slipped on some grease on the floor and fell to the side, out of the way of the falling tool.
6. Mr. Brown tried to avoid Mr. Smith as he fell. In so doing, he fell against some pipes which were leaning against the wall. The pipes fell on both Mr. Brown and Mr. Smith

Mr. Smith and Mr. Brown were both badly bruised and shaken. They were sent to the General Hospital to determine if any bones were broken. The office was later notified that neither employee was seriously hurt.

Since the accident, matters relating to safety and accident prevention around the shop have occupied the staff. There have been a number of complaints about the location of tools and equipment. Several employees are reluctant to work in the shop unless conditions are improved. Please advise as to the best way to handle this situation.

1. The one of the following which it is MOST important to add to the above memorandum is   1._____

    A. a signature line
    B. a transmittal note
    C. the date of the memo
    D. the initials of the typist

2. The MOST logical order in which to list the circumstances relative to the accident is   2.

    A. as shown (1, 2, 3, 4, 5, 6)   B. 2, 3, 1, 5, 4, 6
    C. 1, 5, 4, 6, 3, 2   D. 3, 2, 4, 6, 1, 5

3. The one of the following which does NOT properly belong with the rest of the memorandum is   3. _____

    A. the first section of paragraph 1   B. the list of circumstances
    C. paragraph 2   D. paragraph 3

4. According to the information in the memorandum, the BEST description of the subject is: 4. _____

    A. Effect of accident on work output of the division
    B. Description of accident involving Mr. Smith and Mr. Brown
    C. Recommendations on how to avoid future accidents
    D. Safety and accident control in the shop

Questions 5-10.

DIRECTIONS: A ferry terminal supervisor is asked to write a report on the incident described in the following passage. Questions 5 through 10 are to be answered on the basis of the incident and the supervisor's report. Your answers should be based on the assumption that everything described in the passage is true.

On July 27, a rainy, foggy day, Joseph Jones and Steven Smith were in the Whitehall Ferry Terminal at about 9:50 A.M. waiting for the 10:00 A.M. ferry to Staten Island. Smith, seated with his legs stretched out in the aisle, was reading the sports page of the DAILY NEWS. Jones was walking by, drinking ginger ale from a cup. Neither man paid any attention to the other until Jones tripped over Smith's foot, fell to the floor, and dropped his drink. Smith looked at Jones as he lay on the floor and burst out laughing. Jones, infuriated, got up and punched Smith in the jaw. The force of the blow drove Smith's head back against the bench on which he was sitting. Smith did not fight back; he appeared to be dazed. Bystanders called a terminal worker, who assisted in making Smith as comfortable as possible.

One of the other people waiting in the terminal for the ferry was a nurse, who examined Smith and told the ferry terminal supervisor that Smith probably had a concussion. An ambulance was called to take Smith to the hospital. A policeman arrived on the scene.

Jones' injury consisted of a sprained ankle and some bruises, but he refused medical attention. Jones explained to the supervisor what had happened. Jones truly regretted what he had done and went to the local police station with the policeman.

5. Of the following facts about the above incident, which one would be MOST important to include in the ferry terminal supervisor's report?   5. _____

    A. The time the next boat was due to arrive
    B. Jones was carrying a cup of ginger ale
    C. Smith was sitting with his legs stretched out in the aisle
    D. Why Smith and Jones were in the terminal

6. The MAIN purpose of writing a report of the above incident is to   6._____

    A. make recommendations for preventing fights in the terminal
    B. state the important facts of the incident
    C. blame Jones for not looking where he was going
    D. provide evidence that Smith was not at fault

7. An adequate report of the above incident MUST give the names of the participants, the   7._____
names of witnesses, and the

    A. date, the place, the time, and the events that took place
    B. date, the events that took place, the time, and the names of the terminal personnel
on duty that day
    C. place, the names of the terminal personnel on duty that day, the weather conditions, and the events which took place
    D. names of the passengers in the terminal, the time, the place, and the events which took place

8. The supervisor asked for individuals who had witnessed the entire incident to give their   8._____
account of what they had seen. Thomas White, a twelve-year-old boy said that Jones fell,
got up, turned, and then hit Smith.
Thomas White's description of the incident is

    A. *adequate;* it is truthful, straight-forward, and includes necessary details
    B. *adequate;* it shows that the incident was not started on purpose
    C. *inadequate;* he is too young to understand the implications of his testimony
    D. *inadequate;* it omits certain pertinent facts about the incident

9. Another witness, Mary Collins, told the ferry terminal supervisor that when she heard   9._____
Jones fall, she looked in that direction and saw Jones get up and hit Smith, who was
laughing. She immediately ran to find a terminal worker to prevent further fighting. When
she returned, she found Smith slumped on the bench. Mrs. Collins' report is USEFUL
because

    A. it proves that Smith antagonized Jones
    B. it indicates that Jones beat Smith repeatedly
    C. she witnessed that Jones hit Smith
    D. it shows that only one punch was thrown

10. Based on the description given above, which of the following would be the MOST accurate summary for the ferry terminal supervisor to put in his report?   10._____

    A. Jones fell and Smith laughed, which caused Jones to beat him until bystanders got
a terminal worker to separate them.
    B. Smith was reading a newspaper when Jones fell. Then Jones hit Smith and dazed
him. Smith was examined by a nurse who said that Smith had a serious concussion.
    C. Jones tripped accidentally over Smith's legs and fell. Smith laughed at Jones, who
lost his temper and hit Smith, driving Smith's head against the back of a bench.
    D. Smith antagonized Jones first, by tripping him second, by laughing at him, and third
by not fighting back. Smith was aided by a nurse and went to the hospital.

Questions 11-13.

DIRECTIONS: Questions 11 through 13 are to be answered SOLELY on the basis of the following report.

To: John Greene   Date: May 5
           General Park Foreman

From: Earl Jones   Subject:
           Gardener

   On May 3rd, as I was finishing a job six feet from the boat-house, I observed that the hole which had been filled in last week was now not level with the ground around it. This seems to be a hazardous condition because it might cause pedestrians to fall into it. I, therefore, suggest that this job be redone as soon as possible.

11. This report should be considered poorly written MAINLY because   11._____

     A.   it does not give enough information to take appropriate action
     B.   too many different tenses are used
     C.   it describes no actual personal injury to anyone
     D.   there is no recommendation in the report to remedy the situation

12. It is noted that the subject of the report has been left out.   12._____
     Which of the following statements would be BEST as the subject of this report?

     A.   Observation made by Earl Jones, Gardener
     B.   Deteriorating condition of park grounds
     C.   Report of dangerous condition near boathouse
     D.   A dangerous walk through the park

13. In order for John Greene to take appropriate action, additional information should be 13._____
     added to the report giving the

     A.   exact date the repair was made
     B.   exact location of the hole
     C.   exact time the observation was made
     D.   names of the crew who previously filled in the hole

Questions 14-18.

DIRECTIONS: Questions 14 through 18 consist of sets of four sentences lettered A, B, C, and
              For each question, choose the sentence which is grammatically and stylistically MOST appropriate for use in a formal written report.

14. A. It is recommended, therefore, that the impasse panel hearings are to be convened on September 30.   14.____
     B. It is therefore recommended that the impasse panel hearings be convened on September 30.
     C. Therefore, it is recommended to convene the impasse panel hearings on September 30.
     D. It is recommended that the impasse panel hearings therefore should be convened on September 30.

15. A. Penalties have been assessed for violating the Taylor Law by several unions.   15.____
     B. When they violated provisions of the Taylor Law, several unions were later penalized.
     C. Several unions have been penalized for violating provisions of the Taylor Law.
     D. Several unions' violating provisions of the Taylor Law resulted in them being penalized.

16. A. The number of disputes settled through mediation has increased significantly over the past two years.   16.____
     A. The number of disputes settled through mediation are increasing significantly over two-year periods.
     B. Over the past two years, through mediation, the number of disputes settled increased significantly.
     C. There is a significant increase over the past two years of the number of disputes settled through mediation.

17. A. The union members will vote to determine if the contract is to be approved.   17.____
     B. It is not yet known whether the union members will ratify the proposed contract.
     C. When the union members vote, that will determine the new contract.
     D. Whether the union members will ratify the proposed contract, it is not yet known.

18. A. The parties agreed to an increase in fringe benefits in return for greater worker productivity.   18.____
     A. Greater productivity was agreed to be provided in return for increased fringe benefits.
     B. Productivity and fringe benefits are interrelated; the higher the former, the more the latter grows.
     C. The contract now provides that the amount of fringe benefits will depend upon the level of output by the workers.

19. Of the following excerpts, selected from letters, the one which is considered by modern letter writing experts to be the BEST is: 19.____

     A. Attached please find the application form to be filled out by you. Return the form to this office at the above address.
     B. Forward to this office your check accompanied by the application form enclosed with this letter.
     C. If you wish to apply, please complete and return the enclosed form with your check.
     D.   In reply to your letter of December _____, enclosed herewith please find the application form you requested.

20. A city employee who writes a letter requesting information from a businessman should realize that, of the following, it is MOST important to   20.____

    A. end the letter with a polite closing
    B. make the letter short enough to fit on one page
    C. use a form, such as a questionnaire, to save the businessman's time
    D. use a courteous tone that will get the desired cooperation

Questions 21-22.

DIRECTIONS: Questions 21 and 22 consist of four sentences. Choose the one sentence in each set of four that would be BEST for a formal letter or report. Consider grammar and appropriate usage.

21.   A. Most all the work he completed before he become ill.   21.____
    B. He completed most of the work before becoming ill.
    C. Prior to him becoming ill his work was mostly completed.
    D. Before he became ill most of the work he had completed.

22.   A. Being that the report lacked a clearly worded recommendation, it did not matter   22.____
    that it contained enough information.
    B. There was enough information in the report, although it, including the recommendation, were not clearly worded.
    C. Although the report contained enough information, it did not have a clearly worded recommendation.
    D. Though the report did not have a recommendation that was clearly worded, and the information therein contained was enough.

Questions 23-25.

DIRECTIONS: In Questions 23 through 25, choose the sentence which is BEST from the point of view of English usage suitable for a business letter or report.

23.   A. Answering of veterans' inquiries, together with the receipt of fees, have been handled by the Bursar's Office since the new President came.   23.____
    B. Since the new President's arrival, the handling of all veteran's inquiries has been turned over to the Bursar's Office.
    C. In addition to the receipt of fees, the Bursar's Office has been handling veterans' inquiries since the new President came.
    D. The principle change in the work of the Bursar's Office since the new President came is that it now handles veterans' inquiries as well as the receipt of fees.

24.   A. The current unrest about education undoubtedly stems in part from the fact that the people fear the basic purposes of the schools are being neglected or supplanted by spurious ones.   24.____
    B. The fears of people that the basic purposes of the schools are being neglected or supplanted by spurious ones contributes to the current unrest about education.

C. Undoubtedly some responsibility for the current unrest about education must be assigned to peoples' fears that the purpose and base of the school system is being neglected or supplanted.
D. From the fears of people that the basic purposes of the schools are being neglected or supplanted by spurious ones undoubtedly stem in part the current unrest about education.

25. A. The existence of administrative phenomena are clearly established, but their characteristics, relations and laws are obscure.　　25.____
B. The obscurity of the characteristics, relations and laws of administrative phenomena do not preclude their existence.
C. Administrative phenomena clearly exists in spite of the obscurity of their characteristics, relations and laws.
D. The characteristics, relations and laws of administrative phenomena are obscure but the existence of the phenomena is clear.

KEY (CORRECT ANSWERS)

1. C		11. A	
2. B		12. C	
3. D		13. B	
4. B		14. B	
5. C		15. C	
6. B		16. A	
7. A		17. B	
8. D		18. A	
9. C		19. C	
10. C		20. D	

21. B
22. C
23. C
24. A
25. D

TEST 3

DIRECTIONS: Each question or incomplete statement is followed by several suggested answers or completions. Select the one that BEST answers the question or completes the statement. *PRINT THE LETTER OF THE CORRECT ANSWER IN THE SPACE AT THE RIGHT.*

1. Of the following, the BEST statement concerning the placement of *Conclusions and Recommendations* in a management report is: 1.____

   A. Recommendations should always be included in a report unless the report presents the results of an investigation.
   B. If a report presents conclusions, it must present recommendations.
   C. Every statement that is a conclusion should grow out of facts given elsewhere in the report.
   D. Conclusions and recommendations should always conclude the report because they depend on its contents.

2. Assume you are preparing a systematic analysis of your agency's pest control program and its effect on eliminating rodent infestation of premises in a specific region. To omit from your report important facts which you originally received from the person to whom you are reporting is GENERALLY considered to be   2.____

   A. *desirable;* anyone who is likely to read the report can consult his files for extra information
   B. *undesirable;* the report should include major facts that are obtained as a result of your efforts
   C. *desirable;* the person you are reporting to does not pass the report on to others who lack his own familiarity with the subject
   D. *undesirable;* the report should include all of the facts that are obtained as a result of your efforts

3. Of all the non-verbal devices used in report writing, tables are used most frequently to enable a reader to compare statistical information more easily. Hence, it is important that an analyst know when to use tables. Which one of the following statements that relate to tables is generally considered to be LEAST valid?   3.____

   A. A table from an outside source must be acknowledged by the report writer.
   B. A table should be placed far in advance of the point where it is referred to or discussed in the report.
   C. The notes applying to a table are placed at the bottom of the table, rather than at the bottom of the page on which the table is found.
   D. A table should indicate the major factors that effect the data it contains.

4. Assume that an analyst writes reports which contain more detail than might be needed to serve their purpose. Such a practice is GENERALLY considered to be   4.____

   A. *desirable;* this additional detail permits maximized machine utilization
   B. *undesirable;* if specifications of reports are defined when they are first set up, loss of flexibility will follow
   C. *desirable;* everything ought to be recorded so it will be there if it is ever needed
   D. *undesirable;* recipients of these reports are likely to discredit them entirely

Questions 5-6.

DIRECTIONS: Questions 5 and 6 consist of sentences lettered A, B, C, and D. For each question, choose the sentence which is stylistically and grammatically MOST appropriate for a management report.

5.   A.   For too long, the citizen has been forced to rely for his productivity information on   5._____
           the whims, impressions and uninformed opinion of public spokesmen.
      B.   For too long, the citizen has been forced to base his information about productiv-
           ity on the whims, impressions and uninformed opinion of public spokesmen.
      C.   The citizen has been forced to base his information about productivity on the
           whims, impressions and uninformed opinion of public spokesmen for too long.
      D.   The citizen has been forced for too long to rely for his productivity information on
           the whims, impressions and uninformed opinion of public spokesmen.

6.   A.   More competition means lower costs to the city, there- by helping to compensate   6._____
           for inflation.
      B.   More competition, helping to compensate for inflation, means lower costs to the
           city.
      C.   Inflation may be compensated for by more competition, which will reduce the
           city's costs.
      D.   The costs to the city will be lessened by more competition, helping to compen-
           sate for inflation.

Questions 7-11.

DIRECTIONS: In Questions 7 through 11, choose the sentence which is BEST from the point of view of English usage suitable for a business letter or report.

7.   A.   It is the opinion of the Commissioners that programs which include the construc-   7._____
           tion of cut-rate municipal garages in the central business district is inadvisable.
      B.   Having reviewed the material submitted, the program for putting up cut-rate
           garages in the central business district seemed likely to cause traffic congestion.
      C.   The Commissioners believe that putting up cut-rate municipal garages in the
           central business district is inadvisable.
      D.   Making an effort to facilitate the cleaning of streets in the central business dis-
           trict, the building of cut-rate municipal garages presents the problem that it would
           encourage more motorists to come into the central city.

8.   A.   This letter, together with the reports, are to be sent to the principal.   8._____
      B.   The reports, together with this letter, is to be sent to the principal.
      C.   The reports and this letter is to be sent to the principal.
      D.   This letter, together with the reports, is to be sent to the principal.

9.   A.   Each employee has to decide for themselves whether to take the examination.   9._____
      B.   Each of the employees has to decide for himself whether to take the examina-
           tion.
      C.   Each of the employees has to decide for themselves whether to take the exami-
           nation.
      D.   Each of the employees have to decide for himself whether to take the examina-
           tion.

10. A. The reason a new schedule is being prepared is that there has been a change in priorities.   10.____
     B. Because there has been a change in priorities is the reason why a new schedule is being made up.
     C. The reason why a new schedule is being made up is because there has been a change in priorities.
     D. Because of a change in priorities is the reason why a new schedule is being prepared.

11. A. The changes in procedure had an unfavorable affect upon the output of the unit.   11.____
     B. The increased output of the unit was largely due to the affect of the procedural changes.
     C. The changes in procedure had the effect of increasing the output of the unit.
     D. The increased output of the unit from the procedural changes were the effect.

Questions 12-19.

DIRECTIONS: Questions 12 through 19 each consist of four sentences. Choose the one sentence in each set of four that would be BEST for a formal letter or report. Consider grammar and appropriate usage.

12. A. These statements can be depended on, for their truth has been guaranteed by reliable city employees.   12.____
     B. Reliable city employees guarantee the facts with regards to the truth of these statements.
     C. Most all these statements have been supported by city employees who are reliable and can be depended upon.
     D. The city employees which have guaranteed these statements are reliable.

13. A. I believe the letter was addressed to either my associate or I.   13.____
     B. If properly addressed, the letter will reach my associate and I.
     C. My associate's name, as well as mine, was on the letter.
     D. The letter had been addressed to myself and my associate.

14. A. The secretary would have corrected the errors if she knew that the supervisor would see the report.   14.____
     B. The supervisor reprimanded the secretary, whom she believed had made careless errors.
     C. Many errors were found in the report which she typed and could not disregard them.
     D. The errors in the typed report were so numerous that they could hardly be overlooked.

15. A. His consultant was as pleased as he with the success of the project.   15.____
     B. The success of the project pleased both his consultant and he.
     C. He and also his consultant was pleased with the success of the project.
     D. Both his consultant and he was pleased with the success of the project.

16.
   A. Since the letter did not contain the needed information, it was not real useful to him.
   B. Being that the letter lacked the needed information, he could not use it.
   C. Since the letter lacked the needed information, it was of no use to him.
   D. This letter was useless to him because there was no needed information in it.

16.____

17.
   A. Scarcely had the real estate tax increase been declared than the notices were sent out.
   B. They had no sooner declared the real estate tax increases when they sent the notices to the owners.
   C. The city had hardly declared the real estate tax increase till the notices were prepared for mailing.
   D. No sooner had the real estate tax increase been declared than the notices were sent out.

17.____

18.
   A. Though deeply effected by the setback, the advice given by the admissions office began to seem more reasonable.
   B. Although he was deeply effected by the setback, the advice given by the admissions office began to seem more reasonable.
   C. Though the setback had affected him deeply, the advise given by the admissions office began to seem more reasonable.
   D. Although he was deeply affected by the setback, the advice given by the admissions office began to seem more reasonable.

18.____

19.
   A. Returning to the administration building after attendance at a meeting, the door was locked despite an agreement that it would be left open.
   B. When he returned to the administration building after attending a meeting, he found the door locked, despite an agreement that it would be left open.
   C. After attending a meeting, the door to the administration building was locked, despite an agreement that it would be left open.
   D. When he returned to the administration building after attendance at a meeting, he found the door locked, despite an agreement that it would be left open.

19.____

20. A formal business report may consist of many parts, including the following:
   1. Table of Contents
   2. List of references
   3. Preface
   4. Index
   5. List of tables
   6. Conclusions or recommendations
Of the following, in setting up a formal report, the PROPER order of the six parts listed is:

   A. 1, 3, 6, 5, 2, 4   B. 4, 3, 2, 5, 6, 1
   C. 3, 1, 5, 6, 2, 4   D. 2, 5, 3, 1, 4, 6

20.____

21. Suppose you are writing a report on an interview you have just completed with a particu- 21._____
larly hostile applicant for public assistance.
Which of the following BEST describes what you should include in this report?

    A. What you think caused the applicant's hostile attitude during the interview
    B. Specific examples of the applicant's hostile remarks and behavior
    C. The relevant information uncovered during the interview
    D. A recommendation that the applicant's request be denied because of his hostility

22. When including recommendations in a report to your supervisor, which of the following is 22._____
MOST important for you to do?

    A. Provide several alternative courses of action for each recommendation.
    B. First present the supporting evidence, then the recommendations.
    C. First present the recommendations, then the supporting evidence.
    D. Make sure the recommendations arise logically out of the information in the report.

23. It is often necessary that the writer of a report present facts and sufficient arguments to 23._____
gain acceptance of the points, conclusions, or recommendations set forth in the report.
Of the following, the LEAST advisable step to take in organizing a report, when such
argumentation is the important factor, is a(n)

    A. elaborate expression of personal belief
    B. businesslike discussion of the problem as a whole
    C. orderly arrangement of convincing data
    D. reasonable explanation of the primary issues

24. Assume that a clerk is asked to prepare a special report which he has not prepared 24._____
before. He decides to make a written outline of the report before writing it in full. This
decision by the clerk is

    A. *good,* mainly because it helps the writer to organize his thoughts and decide what
will go into the report
    B. *good,* mainly because it clearly shows the number of topics, number of pages, and
the length of the report
    C. *poor,* mainly because it wastes the time of the writer since he will have to write the
full report anyway
    D. *poor,* mainly because it confines the writer to those areas listed in the outline

25. Assume that a clerk in the water resources central shop is asked to prepare an impor- 25._____
tant report, giving the location and condition of various fire hydrants in the city. One of
the hydrants in question is broken and is spewing rusty water in the street, creating a
flooded condition in the area. The clerk reports that the hydrant is broken but does not
report the escaping water or the flood.
Of the following, the BEST evaluation of the clerk's decision about what to report is that
it is basically

    A. *correct;* chiefly because a lengthy report would contain irrelevant information
    B. *correct;* chiefly because a more detailed description of a hydrant should be made
by a fireman, not a clerk
    C. *incorrect;* chiefly because the clerk's assignment was to describe the condition of
the hydrant and he should give a full explanation
    D. *incorrect;* chiefly because the clerk should include as much information as possible
in his report whether or not it is relevant

KEY (CORRECT ANSWERS)

1.	C		11.	C
2.	B		12.	A
3.	B		13.	C
4.	D		14.	D
5.	B		15.	A
6.	A		16.	C
7.	C		17.	D
8.	D		18.	D
9.	B		19.	B
10.	A		20.	C

21.	C
22.	D
23.	A
24.	A
25.	C

EXAMINATION SECTION
TEST 1

DIRECTIONS: Each question or incomplete statement is followed by several suggested answers or completions. Select the one that BEST answers the question or completes the statement. *PRINT THE LETTER OF THE CORRECT ANSWER IN THE SPACE AT THE RIGHT.*

1. From the public relations standpoint, it is an indisputable fact that public employees may please by an attitude of courtesy and helpfulness or may irritate by an attitude of superiority and a show of authority.
According to this statement only, it may BEST be said that   1.____

    A. all public employees are public relations agents whether they realize it or not
    B. every department should have a public relations division to handle public contacts
    C. good public relations can best be maintained through means other than personal contact
    D. the matter of good public relations is the most important function of a city department

2. In regard to the public employee, the average citizen is not interested in time and heavy work schedules. When the average citizen needs assistance, and the public employee fails to serve him promptly and successfully, he estimates the efficiency of the entire service accordingly.
According to the above statement, the average citizen judges the public service by the   2.____

    A. absence or prevalence of public works activities in his neighborhood
    B. amount of work a public employee does in a given time
    C. economies leading to lowered taxes which are put in effect
    D. response of a public employee when he asks for help

3. The foreman should never fail to recognize that a man has a perfect right to come to him with a grievance. In fact, that is an important part of every foreman's job. That is why management places men in foremanship positions–so that they are always available to men in the ranks for questions, complaints, suggestions, and information.
Grievance situations are inevitable wherever men work together.
On the basis of the above statement only, it may BEST be said that   3.____

    A. a foreman should not allow a man to present a grievance when he quite evidently comes in with a *chip on his shoulder*
    B. an alert and competent foreman can correct conditions and remove causes before a grievance situation develops
    C. differences of opinion and injured feelings cannot be avoided where men work together
    D. where good morale exists in a crew of competent workmen, differences of opinion are not inevitable

4. Physical fitness is not the only requirement of the successful foreman. His moral charac-   4.____
ter must be such as to withstand the most severe tests. His word must be as good as his
bond.
According to the above statement, a foreman MUST be

    A.   as intelligent as he is physically fit
    B.   bonded before he can be appointed
    C.   trustworthy in every respect
    D.   wise enough to handle difficult situations successfully

5. Sometimes in the performance of his duties, a foreman must act alone, without advice of   5.____
his superior and without reference to any books or other authority for guidance. According to this statement only, a foreman must, in the exercise of his duties, sometimes be

    A.   active   B.   cautious
    C.   self–reliant   D.   stern

6. A foreman should never underestimate the importance of detail. It is the basis of suc-   6.____
cess. He will not succeed if he thinks it a big nuisance, has no desire to master it, or fails
to see that big things are but pyramids built up of little things.
According to this statement only, it may BEST be said that

    A.   details are little things that are always nuisances
    B.   details command most of a foreman's attention
    C.   mastery of detail means success
    D.   pyramids are, in reality, little things

7. A foreman is the contact man between top management and the worker, and it is part of   7.____
his job to secure compliance with departmental rules and regulations through the maximum utilization of persuasion and education and the minimum application of coercion.
According to the above statement only, a foreman should

    A.   employ an equal mixture of education and coercion in securing compliance with
         departmental rules and regulations
    B.   never use the threat of discipline to secure conformance with departmental rules
         and regulations
    C.   preferably use the threat of discipline to secure conformance with departmental
         rules and regulations
    D.   seek to obtain voluntary compliance with departmental rules and regulations

8. Records form the cumulative memory of an organization, and the speed and certainty   8.____
with which they can be made available is a vital factor in doing a job. Even in a small unit,
the memory of an individual or of a group of persons cannot safely be depended upon for
accuracy and completeness of information.
According to this statement only, it may BEST be said that

    A.   a good memory is always a reliable memory with respect to accuracy and com-
         pleteness of information
    B.   records are not necessary if there is a foreman or mechanic on the job with a
         remarkable memory
    C.   records are of absolutely no use unless they are accurate and completely informa-
         tive
    D.   the memory of persons cannot compete with records for accuracy and complete-
         ness of information

9. Conscientious work on the job stems not necessarily from right thinking but often from good habits. However, the conduct on the job to be most admired is dictated, not by the desire to secure the foreman's approval and avoid disciplining, but by the desire to do what is right because it is felt and believed to be right; in short, from a sense of duty. According to the above statement only, it may BEST be said that

    9.____

    A. a desire to secure the foreman's approval prompts the highest type of conduct on the job
    B. a sense of duty is the basis for the most commendable action on the job
    C. it is wrong to act on a job without regard for the foreman's approval
    D. there can be absolutely no excuse for misconduct on the job

10. A foreman's continuous and periodic checking of a mechanic's work will keep it safe and free from error but will also impede its rapid finish. This continuous checking serves the cause of order but not of progress.
According to this statement only, it may BEST be said that

    10.____

    A. a foreman's check on a mechanic's work, while serving a useful purpose, also has a disadvantage
    B. a foreman must choose between doing a job rapidly or in a safe and orderly manner
    C. rapid completion of a job is under all circumstances most preferable
    D. there can be no progress in doing a job unless all checking is done away with

11. In enforcing compliance with safety regulations, a foreman should take the attitude that regulations must be complied with because

    11.____

    A. accident prevention is a recent development in motor vehicle work and still in the experimental stage
    B. compliance with safety regulations will make other safety precautions unnecessary
    C. safety regulations are based on reason and experience with the best methods of accident prevention
    D. they are regulations of the department which must be obeyed without question as an end in itself

12. It has been found that controlled rest periods during the work day

    12.____

    A. *lower* the quality of the finished work
    B. *reduce* fatigue and increase output
    C. *reduce* fatigue and have no effect on output
    D. *reduce* fatigue and reduce output

13. Of the following, a foreman's MOST important function is to

    13.____

    A. assume responsibility for his men's errors
    B. develop and maintain cordial relations with his men
    C. gauge and record his men's efficiency
    D. guide and evaluate his men's work

14. In general, the number of mechanics that one foreman can effectively supervise is LARGEST when his men are   14.____

    A. assigned a limited number of widely varied jobs
    B. assigned simple and repetitive jobs
    C. given opportunity to use their own initiative
    D. required to meet high work standards

15. The one of the following that is a sound principle of good foremanship is that   15.____

    A. assignment of jobs should be made impartially without regard for personalities of the individuals involved
    B. delegation of authority for a job to a subordinate does not relieve the foreman of responsibility
    C. loss of time can be avoided by having the foreman make all decisions without consulting the men
    D. the organizational structure or set-up of a working crew should be rigid rather than flexible

16. In assigning his men to various jobs, the BEST principle for a foreman to follow is to   16.____

    A. assign each of them to a job and let them adjust to it in their own way in all respects
    B. assume that men appointed to the position can do all parts of the work equally well
    C. rotate a man from job to job until you find one which he can do
    D. study his men's abilities and assign them accordingly

17. A mechanic to whom you, as the foreman, have given detailed instructions on how to do a job tells you some of the steps are unnecessary. Of the following, the BEST procedure for you to follow is to   17.____

    A. insist that the mechanic carry out your instructions as given so that your authority is not disregarded
    B. investigate the mechanic's statements and if they are valid, issue new instructions
    C. point out that you don't have enough time to justify and explain all the instructions you give
    D. tell him that because of your longer experience, your method is more likely to be right rather than his

18. In assigning a newly appointed, well-qualified mechanic, the BEST one of the following methods which the foreman should follow is to   18.____

    A. assign a large variety of jobs to this man at one time so that he can get an overall picture of the position as rapidly as possible
    B. assign one definite job to the mechanic and have him continue to perform this task until it is done perfectly, regardless of the time involved
    C. explain the duties, emphasizing those to which the mechanic will be first assigned and give him new tasks when reasonable proficiency in the earlier assignment is attained
    D. tell the mechanic of the types of work to be done and then, since he is supposedly well-qualified, let him employ the methods he desires with no further supervision

19. As a foreman, you must assign a job of considerable difficulty to your normally efficient   19.____
crew. Of the following, you are MOST likely to achieve successful results and a cooperative attitude on the part of your men if you

    A. give careful directions on only one step of the job at a time and provide further
directions only as necessary
    B. provide a complete set of instructions which each member of the crew is to follow
with no deviations
    C. present an accurate comprehensive outline of the work, explaining in some detail
the responsibility of each mechanic
    D. outline the work briefly and permit each mechanic to use his own initiative and
judgment in doing his job

20. If a foreman asks his mechanics for suggestions, they will MOST probably   20.____

    A. assume that the foreman is not capable of filling his job
    B. refuse to make any suggestions since they are not receiving foreman's pay
    C. resent having these additional duties and responsibilities thrust upon them
    D. work better since they feel they are making a helpful contribution to the work

---

KEY (CORRECT ANSWERS)

1.	A	11.	C
2.	D	12.	B
3.	C	13.	D
4.	C	14.	B
5.	C	15.	B
6.	C	16.	D
7.	D	17.	B
8.	D	18.	C
9.	B	19.	C
10.	A	20.	D

TEST 2

DIRECTIONS: Each question or incomplete statement is followed by several suggested answers or completions. Select the one that BEST answers the question or completes the statement. *PRINT THE LETTER OF THE CORRECT ANSWER IN THE SPACE AT THE RIGHT.*

1. Four weeks after you have been appointed a foreman, you believe you have discovered a better way of doing a job. Of the following, the BEST thing for you to do is to   1.____

   A. discuss your plan with other foremen and be guided by their judgment
   B. explain your idea to your superior at a favorable opportunity
   C. try out your plan before talking it over with anyone
   D. wait until you are asked for suggestions and then come forward with your idea

2. In disciplining men, the BEST of the following principles for a foreman to follow is to   2.____

   A. administer disciplinary measures calmly and apply penalties impartially as individual cases warrant
   B. *bawl* the crew out as a group periodically to keep the men in line and prevent disregard of rules
   C. criticize his men immediately as soon as they do something wrong and show that he is angry so that they will remember it
   D. reprimand them sharply when they deserve it so that others can hear it and will watch their step

3. The BEST practice for a foreman to follow in handling a mechanic's grievance is to   3.____

   A. delay hearing it in the hope the man will forget it
   B. hear it and settle it as promptly as possible
   C. hear it only if it is important
   D. refuse to hear it since a foreman is a part of management

4. Of the following incentives for a mechanic to do his work well, the one which is generally accepted as being MOST effective is to   4.____

   A. assure the mechanic that his efforts will be recognized and appreciated
   B. have a close inspection system which will detect any sub–standard work
   C. have a rigid discipline with suspension, demotion, or discharge as penalties
   D. keep the mechanic on his toes by not letting him know how he stands with his superiors

5. Assume a new policy is being put into effect and you, as the foreman, are responsible for seeing that your men understand and accept it.
   Of the following, your BEST procedure is to   5.____

   A. describe in detail how the new policy will be carried out and the disciplinary measures to be used in enforcing it
   B. discuss the new policy with your men, let them tell you their opinions and encourage them to make plans to carry it out
   C. give your men a mimeographed or typed notice containing all essential elements of the new policy and let it go at that
   D. have a personal interview with each of your mechanics in private to tell him of the new policy and how it will affect him

6. If one of your mechanics does an exceptionally fine piece of work, it would be BEST for
   you, as the foreman, to

   6.____

   A. praise him moderately for the work he has done so that he knows his efforts are
      appreciated
   B. tell him in front of the other members of the crew that none of the other mechanics
      could possibly have done that good a job
   C. say nothing to him to forestall any possibility that he will become complacent and
      rest on his laurels
   D. explain to him how the job could have been improved to prevent his becoming con-
      ceited

7. Of the following actions by a foreman, the one which will MOST likely improve the work of
   a mechanic is

   7.____

   A. to have a discussion of common errors and a question and answer period in group
      staff meetings
   B. a public, immediate, and strong reprimand for every instance of poor performance
   C. to explain the significance of errors made, their results, and methods of improve-
      ment
   D. to have a rigid, impersonal, and subjective application of the service rating system
      for both good and poor performance

8. One of your mechanics is efficient but continually complains about the amount of work he
   has to do. You have noticed that his complaints have a bad effect on the other men.
   As foreman, it would be BEST for you to

   8.____

   A. ask the other men to overlook his complaints because of his efficiency
   B. give him even more work as a disciplinary measure
   C. have a private talk with him and ask him to change his attitude
   D. take some of his work away even if he then does less than the others

9. One of your mechanics turns in a poor piece of work. You, as the foreman, tell him it is
   completely unsatisfactory and he will have to do better work in the future. This procedure, from the standpoint of good foremanship, is

   9.____

   A. *desirable,* because the mechanic was given a chance to explain why his work was
      poor
   B. *desirable,* because you are letting the mechanic know just where he *stands* without
      any doubt
   C. *undesirable,* because an interval of time should be permitted to intervene before
      reprimands of this type are delivered
   D. *undesirable,* since a favorable comment should, if possible, be made to him at the
      same time that fault is found with his work

10. Of the following essentials regarding a record-keeping system, the one which would be
    MOST valuable to a foreman is that the system should

    10.____

    A. be in such form that it can be appropriately filed in looseleaf binders
    B. be such that it can be used to show a trend or make comparisons
    C. be simple enough for all mechanics to read and understand
    D. contain a cost figure showing the day-by-day expense of the current job

11. The FIRST step required of a foreman in the process of good job planning is   11._____

    A. determination of what operations are necessary
    B. establishment of production standards
    C. consideration of subcontracting of work
    D. proper layout of physical space and equipment

12. Assume that you are a foreman and have a crew of men working on a job which must be   12._____
completed in two weeks. You believe the deadline cannot be met unless the crew is
increased in number.
Of the following information, the one which would be MOST useful in determining how
many additional men are needed to complete the job in the given time is

    A. a job specification for each man in the crew
    B. the amount of space available as a working area
    C. the crew's present production records
    D. the pooled opinions of your crew and yourself

13. As a foreman, you recommend to your superior the purchase of a new piece of machin-   13._____
ery. The department approves your recommendation. Subsequently, one of your men
tells you he can build a machine which will answer your needs for about half the cost of
the one to be purchased.
Of the following, you should

    A. ask your man for a detailed description of his plan and discuss with your superior
the advisability of building the machine
    B. tell him you cannot permit your men to use machinery which is neither approved
nor standard
    C. tell your man to go ahead and build the machine, with the intention of trying it out
secretly before saying anything about it
    D. tell your man you will consider his suggestion, but in the meantime you go ahead
and order the new piece of machinery

14. Assume that as foreman you find that some of your mechanics are being assigned work   14._____
directly by your superior.
Of the following, it would be BEST for you to

    A. appoint one mechanic in your crew to do all this extra work assigned directly by
your superior, leaving the others free to do your work
    B. instruct your mechanics to give precedence to this extra work whenever your supe-
rior assigns it
    C. instruct your mechanics to report to you whenever this extra work is assigned so
that you can determine which has precedence
    D. point out to your superior that it is confusing for a mechanic to have jobs assigned
to him by two persons

15. Of the following, the BEST way for a foreman to improve the morale of his mechanics is   15._____
to

    A. let him know that your superior is informed of a meritorious job
    B. refrain from checking up on them during the course of their work
    C. refrain from telling the shop superintendent about a substandard job
    D. permit the men to take frequent coffee breaks and to smoke on the job

16. When a foreman says that a job was <u>anticipated,</u> he means that it was MOST NEARLY   16.____

    A. avoided   B. delayed
    C. discovered   D. expected

17. A foreman who gives <u>concise</u> orders gives orders which are MOST NEARLY   17.____

    A. ambiguous   B. clear   C. lengthy   D. short

18. If a foreman says that some machinery is being destroyed by <u>friction,</u> it means that it is   18.____
MOST likely being destroyed by

    A. evolution   B. resistance
    C. rotation   D. speed

19. To say that a foreman is <u>lenient</u> means that he is MOST NEARLY   19.____

    A. kind   B. not severe
    C. prejudiced   D. unbiased

20. If a foreman were to <u>salvage</u> some equipment, this means MOST NEARLY that it would   20.____
be

    A. lost   B. overhauled
    C. repaired   D. saved

KEY (CORRECT ANSWERS)

1.	B	11.	A
2.	A	12.	C
3.	B	13.	A
4.	A	14.	D
5.	B	15.	A
6.	A	16.	D
7.	C	17.	D
8.	C	18.	B
9.	D	19.	B
10.	B	20.	D

EXAMINATION SECTION
TEST 1

DIRECTIONS: Each question or incomplete statement is followed by several suggested answers or completions. Select the one that BEST answers the question or completes the statement. *PRINT THE LETTER OF THE CORRECT ANSWER IN THE SPACE AT THE RIGHT.*

1. One of your subordinates, whom you consider to be a troublemaker because of his poor attitude toward his work, has been complaining to other employees about his work and stirring them up to make similar complaints. For you to respond to his actions discreetly and impersonally without any show of emotion or upset is considered to be   1._____

    A. *good* practice; you may change his attitudes for the better
    B. *good* practice; he may be so frustrated by your reaction that he will request a transfer
    C. *poor* practice; other employees may follow his example and choose him as their spokesman
    D. *poor* practice; he may not know how to respond to your lack of emotion

2. The practice of a foreman's requesting his subordinates to submit suggestions regarding ways of reducing costs is   2._____

    A. *inadvisable;* reducing costs is the foreman's responsibility, not that of his subordinates
    B. *inadvisable* he may waste a great deal of time by having to review worthless suggestions
    C. *advisable;* it will give subordinates something to do when they have no work to occupy them
    D. *advisable;* asking subordinates for ideas on cost reduction will make them feel more involved in the work process

3. Of the following, which is the BEST way to store steel pipe and other similarly shaped metal pieces?   3._____

    A. Stack in layers, with alternating rows of materials placed lengthwise and widthwise
    B. Stack in a pyramid shape, with sheets of wood placed between the layers
    C. Stack in layers, with strips of iron, the ends of which are turned up, placed between the layers
    D. In vertical rows, upright against a wall

4. Which one of the following is NOT a usual hazard of handling and servicing storage batteries?   4._____

    A. Acid burns   B. Bruised knuckles
    C. Lead poisoning   D. Electric shock

5. As a foreman, at which point should you report an employee to your superior for working in an unsafe manner?   5._____

    A. The first time he does something that endangers himself or another employee
    B. Usually not at all; this is a matter that should be handled by the foreman
    C. When you become aware of a pattern of unsafe operations in his work
    D. When an accident occurs

6. In order to prevent a fire, oily work rags should be   6._____

    A. kept in covered metal containers
    B. kept in neat piles in a well-ventilated area
    C. kept in open storage boxes, at least ten feet away from any flammable material
    D. wrapped in newspaper and stacked neatly against a fireproof wall

7. For which one of the following uses would it be UNSAFE to use a carpenter's hammer?   7._____
Striking a

    A. casing nail   B. hand punch
    C. hardened steel surface   D. plastic surface

8. When a certain gasoline tank is filled to capacity, it holds 420 gallons.   8._____
If it is 3/4 full, the number of gallons of gasoline it is holding is

    A. 280   B. 315   C. 360   D. 375

9. Eight men working full time take 16 days to do a job. How long should it take if four men   9._____
do this job? _____ days.

    A. 26   B. 28   C. 32   D. 38

10. If 20 feet of lumber costs $62.00, the cost of 45 feet would be   10._____

    A. $136.25   B. $139.50   C. $144.25   D. $149.50

11.   11._____

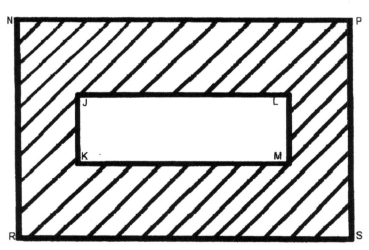

Shown above is a rectangle (JKLM) inside another rectangle (NPSR). What is the area of the shaded portion if LM measures 20 feet, JL measures 30 feet, NR measures 45 feet, and RS measures 55 feet?
_____ square feet.

    A. 600   B. 975   C. 1,875   D. 2,475

12. To produce a certain cleaning compound, four materials, W, X, Y, and Z, are combined by mixing 6 pounds of W, 5 pounds of X, 3 pounds of Y, and 1 pound of Z.
In order to make up 270 pounds of this cleaning compound, the number of pounds of W required is _____ pounds.

    A. 100   B. 108   C. 112   D. 120

12.____

13. The normal work week for a laborer is 35 hours.
If a laborer spends 27 hours at Job Location A and the rest of his work week at Job Location B, the percentage of time spent at Job Location B is MOST NEARLY _____ percent.

    A. 19   B. 21   C. 23   D. 25

13.____

14. Which one of the following is the GENERALLY recommended method of assigning work to your subordinates?

    A. Jobs are given to each man according to his ability to perform the job.
    B. Jobs that take the shortest time are given to the workers with the greatest seniority.
    C. The same amount of work is distributed to each man all of the time.
    D. Least important jobs are given to the less experienced workers.

14.____

15. Which one of the following tasks USUALLY requires two men to work together until the task is completed?

    A. Removing glass partitions from one location and reinstalling them in another
    B. Repairing a leaking faucet
    C. Filling requisitions from stock bins
    D. Clearing walkways of ice and snow

15.____

Questions 16–17.

DIRECTIONS: Questions 16 and 17 are to be answered on the basis of the following report.

To: Al Forbes   Date: March 30
     Director, Building Maintenance
                                Subject:

From: Jim Harris
     Foreman

On March 30, at 10:30 A.M., while working on a piece of sheet metal in the machine shop, Steve Farrell cut his hand so badly that he was rushed to the hospital and required 10 stitches. After the accident, it was determined that Steve had not been wearing gloves when the accident occurred. It is, therefore, suggested that safety procedures for materials handling be reviewed so that an accident such as this may be prevented in the future.

16. The subject of the report has been left out.
Which of the following would be BEST as the subject of this report?

    A. Dangerous Conditions in the Machine Shop
    B. Carelessness of Employees Working in the Machine Shop
    C. Procedures for Handling Accidents
    D. Report of Accident Due to Unsafe Materials Handling

16.____

17. Of the following, this report is unsatisfactory because it omits   17.____

    A. a recommendation for disciplinary action against Steve Farrell
    B. details regarding how the accident occurred
    C. Steve Farrell's prior accident record
    D. the number of sick days that Steve Farrell has available

18. Suppose an employee under your supervision appears to be developing the habit of   18.____
wandering off for a half-hour or more almost every afternoon without offering any
explanation.
The FIRST thing you should do in this situation is to

    A. assign extra work to the employee so that he will have no time to wander off
    B. reprimand the employee officially and give him a copy of the reprimand
    C. transfer the employee to another type of work and observe if his behavior remains
the same
    D. talk to the employee about the reasons why he is leaving the job site

19. Of the following, the MAIN advantage of having one employee responsible for the issu-   19.____
ance of tools is

    A. it assures that the right tool will be used for a particular job
    B. tools will be less likely to be damaged
    C. it insures accountability for the tools
    D. it discourages the use of an employee's personal tools

20. After being inspected, a new ladder is usually coated with a preservative such as clear   20.____
varnish.
Of the following, the MAIN reason for using a clear preservative is that

    A. the name of the department imprinted on the ladder can be easily identified
    B. defects occurring after the inspection can be easily noticed
    C. workers using the ladder are likely to maintain a new ladder in good condition
    D. cracks in the ladder are less likely to occur than if the ladder were painted

KEY (CORRECT ANSWERS)

1. A	11. C
2. D	12. B
3. C	13. C
4. C	14. A
5. C	15. A
6. A	16. D
7. C	17. B
8. B	18. D
9. C	19. C
10. B	20. B

TEST 2

DIRECTIONS: Each question or incomplete statement is followed by several suggested answers or completions. Select the one that BEST answers the question or completes the statement. *PRINT THE LETTER OF THE CORRECT ANSWER IN THE SPACE AT THE RIGHT.*

1. Assume that you, a foreman, expect that some of your workers will have an objection to an order that you must issue.
If it is not an emergency order, it is MOST advisable for you to

    1.____

    A. explain to your workers that you do not agree with the order, but that you have no power to do anything but follow it
    B. issue the order without comment and discourage discussion or objections by your workers
    C. state and explain the order carefully to your workers and allow them time to ask questions and to discuss with you their objections
    D. warn your workers before issuing the order that you will take disciplinary action against anyone who resists carrying out the order

2. On the job, practical jokes have been played frequently upon one particular man under your supervision. When you, as a foreman, ask the reason for such behavior by the men who play these tricks, they say they do this because the victim invites these tricks upon himself.
Of the following, it is MOST appropriate for you, the foreman, to FIRST

    2.____

    A. warn each man involved in such acts that these practical jokes must be discontinued immediately
    B. post a written notice addressed to all the men under your supervision warning them of the dangers involved in playing practical jokes
    C. review the work schedule of your subordinates to see that they have enough work to occupy them for a full day
    D. ask the man on whom the tricks were played if he resents being the victim of such tricks

3. Under which one of the following circumstances would it be BEST for a foreman to give orders in the form of commands rather than requests?
When a foreman

    3.____

    A. is giving orders to one employee directly rather than to the entire crew
    B. is giving orders that require additional instructions as the work progresses
    C. is giving orders to his entire crew to cope with a critical situation
    D. has been ordered by his supervisor to furnish a skeleton crew for holiday work

4. When carrying objects on a two-wheeled handtruck, placing the heavier objects on the bottom of the load is a

    4.____

    A. *good* practice, because the lighter objects are less likely to be damaged
    B. *poor* practice, because the lighter objects are more likely to fall off
    C. *good* practice, because more weight can be loaded on the truck
    D. *poor* practice, because it will be harder to start the truck in motion

5. Of the following, the MAIN advantage in using a Phillips head screw is that   5._____

   A. the threads of the Phillips head screw have a deeper bite than standard screw threads
   B. the screwdriver used on this type of screw is more likely to keep its edge than a standard screwdriver
   C. a single screwdriver fits all size screws of this type
   D. the screwdriver used on this type of screw is less likely to slip than a standard screwdriver

6. One of the reasons why a polyester rope is considered to be the BEST general-purpose   6._____
   rope is that it _____ ropes made of other materials.

   A. does not stretch as much as
   B. is available in longer lengths than
   C. does not fray as much as
   D. contains more strands than

7. A daily inspection tour by the foreman would be of GREATEST benefit to him and his   7._____
   subordinates when the subordinates realize that the foreman

   A. is available to answer any questions they might have about the work
   B. is checking up on them to make certain they are not wasting time
   C. is looking for the type of work that will bring his name to the attention of his superiors
   D. will lend a hand to get the daily work accomplished

8. For you to use different methods of discipline for each employee is considered to be   8._____

   A. *good* practice; each employee should be disciplined in a manner that is most effective for him
   B. *good* practice; your employees will be afraid to misbehave because they can no longer predict your behavior
   C. *poor* practice, employees may consider these different methods a sign of indecisiveness and lose respect for you
   D. *poor* practice; an employee who believes he is getting the harshest discipline may become hostile and antagonistic

9. As a foreman, you have just informed your crew that you want them to follow a new pro-   9._____
   cedure when signing out for tools from the tool cabinet.
   Of the following, the MOST efficient method for you to adopt to make certain that your
   crew is reminded of this new procedure is to

   A. take each man aside and tell him you are counting on him to follow the correct procedure
   B. announce to the men that all tools in the cabinet are stamped with a serial number and the agency name
   C. post instructions for the new procedure at the tool cabinet so the men will be sure to see then when requisitioning tools
   D. question the men at their work sites to learn whether they obtained the tools by following the new procedure

10. For you as a foreman to tell an individual employee how much he is expected to do on a job assignment is a

    10._____

    A. *good* practice, because he will have a goal to try to reach
    B. *bad* practice, because he will be able to determine if you are giving others the same amount of work
    C. *good* practice, because you will be able to give the individual more detailed instructions on how to do the job
    D. *bad* practice, because he will do the minimum amount of work and not be motivated to continue further

11. A laborer who has worked in your agency for five years has just been transferred into your unit.
In order for you to be able to plan his assignments properly, the FIRST thing you should do is to

    11._____

    A. ask him what he already knows about the work handled in your unit
    B. plan a training program for him in which all phases of your unit's operations are covered
    C. assign one of your more experienced laborers to train him in the work of your unit
    D. tell him what you want him to do and then interview him

12. After you have assigned a job to one of your workers, he complains to your superior about the job instead of coming to you with his complaint. He recognizes that it is proper to discuss the complaint with you first. However, he points out that in the past other employees under your supervision have successfully bypassed you with their complaints. Which of the following approaches generally would be MOST productive in getting your subordinates to turn to you first with their complaints?

    12._____

    A. Ask your superior how he handled this complaint, so that you can handle it in the same way when the complaint arises again.
    B. Clarify the steps of the complaint procedure with your employees.
    C. Ask your superior to take no action on the employee complaints, but to refer the employee to you, their supervisor.
    D. Tell your employees that if they do not bring the complaints to you first, they cannot take them to your superior.

13. Of the following, the MAIN reason that on-the-job training is widely used is that

    13._____

    A. the trainee can be producing while he is being trained
    B. the supervisor can assign several trainees to the training at one time
    C. the trainee can progress at his own speed
    D. most supervisors are well-qualified to conduct on-the-job training

14. Of the following, it is BEST for a foreman to begin a new employee's training right after the new employee has

    14.____

    A. made several errors in performing the first task he has been given to do
    B. had an opportunity to meet all the other employees having his title
    C. reported for work in the unit
    D. shown an interest in learning more about the job he has been doing

15. As a foreman, you have always handwritten accident reports. However, a new accident reporting procedure requests that you use a printed form which asks specific questions and provides blank spaces where the information about the accident can be filled in.
Of the following, the MOST important advantage of using this printed form is that

    15.____

    A. the information can be completed by any one of your workers if you are not available
    B. your supervisor can rely on information in a printed form to be more reliable than a completely handwritten report
    C. you can enter as much or as little information on the form as you think necessary
    D. you will be less likely to omit needed information

16. If you replace a blown fuse, and the replaced fuse has burned out shortly thereafter, the FIRST step that should be taken when the replaced fuse has been damaged is that

    16.____

    A. this second fuse should be replaced by a new fuse of the same type and amperage
    B. this second fuse should be replaced by a new fuse of slightly greater amperage
    C. the circuit should be disconnected while the cause of the burn–out is determined
    D. a check of all other fuses at the electrical connection should be made to determine if they were in working order

17. When you are placing a 12-foot portable ladder with a non-slip base against the side of a building, the distance from the base of the ladder to the base of the side of the building should be MOST NEARLY, according to general safety rules, _____ feet.

    17.____

    A. 2   B. 3   C. 4   D. 6

18. A foreman must supply sufficient plywood paneling, each panel measuring 4 feet by 8 feet, to erect a three–sided barrier fence 8 feet high in front of a building entrance. This rectangular area will be closed to the public while the building alterations are made. The longer side of the area measures 24 feet, and each of the shorter sides measures 12 feet.
The MINIMUM number of plywood panels necessary to erect this fence is

    18.____

    A. 9   B. 12   C. 18   D. 24

19. The proper saw to use to cut wood with the grain is a _____ saw.

    19.____

    A. hack   B. crosscut   C. back   D. rip

20. One of your men, Tom Jones, has shown up late for work several times in the past two   20.____
    weeks. The quality of his work, however, is good. This morning, Jones comes in late
    again.
    Of the following, the FIRST action you should take is to

    A. warn Jones that if his lateness continues he will be disciplined
    B. send Jones to the Personnel Officer for disciplinary action
    C. speak to your own supervisor and ask him what to do in this case
    D. ask Jones why he has been arriving late for work so often lately

    _____

KEY (CORRECT ANSWERS)

1.	C	11.	A
2.	A	12.	C
3.	C	13.	A
4.	A	14.	C
5.	D	15.	D
6.	A	16.	C
7.	A	17.	B
8.	A	18.	B
9.	C	19.	D
10.	A	20.	D

_____

EXAMINATION SECTION
TEST 1

DIRECTIONS: Each question or incomplete statement is followed by several suggested answers or completions. Select the one that BEST answers the question or completes the statement. *PRINT THE LETTER OF THE CORRECT ANSWER IN THE SPACE AT THE RIGHT.*

1. Which of the following is the MOST likely action a supervisor should take to help establish an effective working relationship with his departmental superiors?   1.____

    A. Delay the implementation of new procedures received from superiors in order to evaluate their appropriateness.
    B. Skip the chain of command whenever he feels that it is to his advantage.
    C. Keep supervisors informed of problems in his area and the steps taken to correct them.
    D. Don't take up superiors' time by discussing anticipated problems but wait until the difficulties occur.

2. Of the following, the action a supervisor could take which would *generally* be MOST conducive to the establishment of an effective working relationship with employees includes   2.____

    A. maintaining impersonal relationships to prevent development of biased actions
    B. treating all employees equally without adjusting for individual differences
    C. continuous observation of employees on the job with insistence on constant improvement
    D. careful planning and scheduling of work for your employees

3. Which of the following procedures is the LEAST likely to establish effective working relationships between employees and supervisors?   3.____

    A. Encouraging *two-way* communication with employees
    B. Periodic discussion with employees regarding their job performance
    C. Ignoring employees' gripes concerning job difficulties
    D. Avoiding personal prejudices in dealing with employees

4. Criticism can be used as a tool to point out the weak areas of a subordinate's work performance.   4.____
Of the following, the BEST action for a supervisor to take so that his criticism will be accepted is to

    A. focus his criticism on the act instead of on the person
    B. exaggerate the errors in order to motivate the employee to do better
    C. pass judgment quickly and privately without investigating the circumstances of the error
    D. generalize the criticism and not specifically point out the errors in performance

5. In trying to improve the motivation of his subordinates, a supervisor can achieve the BEST results by taking action based upon the assumption that most employees   5.____

    A. have an inherent dislike of work
    B. wish to be closely directed
    C. are more interested in security than in assuming responsibility
    D. will exercise self-direction without coercion

6. When there are conflicts or tensions between top management and lower-level employees in any department, the supervisor should FIRST attempt to

    A. represent and enforce the management point of view
    B. act as the representative of the workers to get their ideas across to management
    C. serve as a two-way spokesman, trying to interpret each side to the other
    D. remain neutral, but keep informed of changes in the situation

6._____

7. A probationary period for new employees is usually provided in many agencies.
The MAJOR purpose of such a period is *usually* to

    A. allow a determination of employee's suitability for the position
    B. obtain evidence as to employee's ability to perform in a higher position
    C. conform to requirements that ethnic hiring goals be met for all positions
    D. train the new employee in the duties of the position

7._____

8. An effective program of orientation for new employees usually includes all of the following EXCEPT

    A. having the supervisor introduce the new employee to his job, outlining his responsibilities and how to carry them out
    B. permitting the new worker to tour the facility or department so he can observe all parts of it in action
    C. scheduling meetings for new employees, at which the job requirements are explained to them and they are given personnel manuals
    D. testing the new worker on his skills and sending him to a centralized in-service workshop

8._____

9. In-service training is an important responsibility of many supervisors.
The MAJOR reason for such training is to

    A. avoid future grievance procedures because employees might say they were not prepared to carry out their jobs
    B. maximize the effectiveness of the department by helping each employee perform at his full potential
    C. satisfy inspection teams from central headquarters of the department
    D. help prevent disagreements with members of the community

9._____

10. There are many forms of useful in-service training. Of the following, the training method which is NOT an appropriate technique for leadership development is to

    A. provide special workshops or clinics in activity skills
    B. conduct institutes to familiarize new workers with the program of the department and with their roles
    C. schedule team meetings for problem-solving, including both supervisors and leaders
    D. have the leader rate himself on an evaluation form periodically

10._____

11. Of the following techniques of evaluating work training programs, the one that is BEST is to   11.____

     A. pass out a carefully designed questionnaire to the trainees at the completion of the program
     B. test the knowledge that trainees have both at the beginning of training and at its completion
     C. interview the trainees at the completion of the program
     D. evaluate performance before and after training for both a control group and an experimental group

12. Assume that a new supervisor is having difficulty making his instructions to subordinates   12.____
clearly understood.
The one of the following which is the FIRST step he should take in dealing with this problem is to

     A. set up a training workshop in communication skills
     B. determine the extent and nature of the communications gap
     C. repeat both verbal and written instructions several times
     D. simplify his written and spoken vocabulary

13. A director has not properly carried out the orders of his assistant supervisor on several   13.____
occasions to the point where he has been successively warned, reprimanded, and
severely reprimanded.
When the director once again does not carry out orders, the PROPER action for the
assistant supervisor to take is to

     A. bring the director up on charges of failing to perform his duties properly
     B. have a serious discussion with the director, explaining the need for the orders and the necessity for carrying them out
     C. recommend that the director be transferred to another district
     D. severely reprimand the director again, making clear that no further deviation will be countenanced

14. A supervisor with several subordinates becomes aware that two of these subordinates   14.____
are neither friendly nor congenial.
In making assignments, it would be BEST for the supervisor to

     A. disregard the situation
     B. disregard the situation in making a choice of assignment but emphasize the need for teamwork
     C. investigate the situation to find out who is at fault and give that individual the less desirable assignments until such time as he corrects his attitude
     D. place the unfriendly subordinates in positions where they have as little contact with one another as possible

15. A DESIRABLE characteristic of a good supervisor is that he should   15.____

     A. identify himself with his subordinates rather than with higher management
     B. inform subordinates of forthcoming changes in policies and programs only when they directly affect the subordinates' activities
     C. make advancement of the subordinates contingent on personal loyalty to the supervisor
     D. make promises to subordinates only when sure of the ability to keep them

16. The supervisor who is MOST likely to be successful is the one who   16.____

    A. refrains from exercising the special privileges of his position
    B. maintains a formal attitude toward his subordinates
    C. maintains an informal attitude toward his subordinates
    D. represents the desires of his subordinates to his superiors

17. Application of sound principles of human relations by a supervisor may be expected to   17.____
_____ the need for formal discipline.

    A. decrease   B. have no effect on
    C. increase   D. obviate

18. The MOST important generally approved way to maintain or develop high morale in   18.____
one's subordinates is to

    A. give warnings and reprimands in a jocular manner
    B. excuse from staff conferences those employees who are busy
    C. keep them informed of new developments and policies of higher management
    D. refrain from criticizing their faults directly

19. In training subordinates, an IMPORTANT principle for the supervisor to recognize is that   19.____

    A. a particular method of instruction will be of substantially equal value for all employees in a given title
    B. it is difficult to train people over 50 years of age because they have little capacity for learning
    C. persons undergoing the same course of training will learn at different rates of speed
    D. training can seldom achieve its purpose unless individual instruction is the chief method used

20. Over an extended period of time, a subordinate is MOST likely to become and remain   20.____
most productive is the supervisor

    A. accords praise to the subordinate whenever his work is satisfactory, withholding criticism except in the case of very inferior work
    B. avoids both praise and criticism except for outstandingly good or bad work performed by the subordinate
    C. informs the subordinate of his shortcomings, as viewed by management, while according praise only when highly deserved
    D. keeps the subordinate informed of the degree of satisfaction with which his performance of the job is viewed by management

KEY (CORRECT ANSWERS)

1.	C	11.	D
2.	D	12.	B
3.	C	13.	A
4.	A	14.	D
5.	D	15.	D
6.	C	16.	D
7.	A	17.	A
8.	D	18.	C
9.	B	19.	C
10.	D	20.	D

———

TEST 2

DIRECTIONS: Each question or incomplete statement is followed by several suggested answers or completions. Select the one that BEST answers the question or completes the statement. *PRINT THE LETTER OF THE CORRECT ANSWER IN THE SPACE AT THE RIGHT.*

1. A supervisor has just been told by a subordinate, Mr. Jones, that another employee, Mr. Smith, deliberately disobeyed an important rule of the department by taking home some confidential departmental material.
   Of the following courses of action, it would be MOST advisable for the supervisor first to

   A. discuss the matter privately with both Mr. Jones and Mr. Smith at the same time
   B. call a meeting of the entire staff and discuss the matter generally without mentioning any employee by name
   C. arrange to supervise Mr. Smith's activities more closely
   D. discuss the matter privately with Mr. Smith

   1.____

2. The one of the following actions which would be MOST efficient and economical for a supervisor to take to minimize the effect of periodic fluctuations in the work load of his unit is to

   A. increase his permanent staff until it is large enough to handle the work of the busy loads
   B. request the purchase of time and labor saving equipment to be used primarily during the busy loads
   C. lower, temporarily, the standards for quality of work performance during peak loads
   D. schedule for the slow periods work that is not essential to perform during the busy periods

   2.____

3. Discipline of employees is usually a. supervisor's responsibility. There may be several useful forms of disciplinary action.
   Of the following, the form that is LEAST appropriate is the

   A. written reprimand or warning
   B. involuntary transfer to another work setting
   C. demotion or suspension
   D. assignment of added hours of work each week

   3.____

4. Of the following, the MOST effective means of dealing with employee disciplinary problems is to

   A. give personality tests to individuals to identify their psychological problems
   B. distribute and discuss a policy manual containing exact rules governing employee behavior
   C. establish a single, clear penalty to be imposed for all wrongdoing irrespective of degree
   D. have supervisors get to know employees well through social mingling

   4.____

5. A recently developed technique for appraising work performance is to have the supervisor record on a continual basis all significant incidents in each subordinate's behavior that indicate unsuccessful action and those that indicate poor behavior.
Of the following, a MAJOR disadvantage of this method of performance appraisal is that it

    A. often leads to overly close supervision
    B. results in competition among those subordinates being evaluated
    C. tends to result in superficial judgments
    D. lacks objectivity for evaluating performance

5.____

6. Assume that you are a supervisor and have observed the performance of an employee during a period of time. You have concluded that his performance needs improvement.
In order to improve his performance, it would, therefore, be BEST for you to

    A. note your findings in the employee's personnel folder so that his behavior is a matter of record
    B. report the findings to the personnel officer so he can take prompt action
    C. schedule a problem-solving conference with the employee
    D. recommend his transfer to simpler duties

6.____

7. When an employee's absences or latenesses seem to be nearing excessiveness, the supervisor should speak with him to find out what the problem is.
Of the following, if such a discussion produces no reasonable explanation, the discussion usually BEST serves to

    A. affirm clearly the supervisor's adherence to proper policy
    B. alert other employees that such behavior is unacceptable
    C. demonstrate that the supervisor truly represents higher management
    D. notify the employee that his behavior is being observed and evaluated

7.____

8. Assume that an employee willfully and recklessly violates an important agency regulation. The nature of the violation is of such magnitude that it demands immediate action, but the facts of the case are not entirely clear. Further, assume that the supervisor is free to make any of the following recommendations.
The MOST appropriate action for the supervisor to take is to recommend that the employee be

    A. discharged   B. suspended
    C. forced to resign   D. transferred

8.____

9. Although employees' titles may be identical, each position in that title may be considerably different.
Of the following, a supervisor should carefully assign each employee to a specific position based PRIMARILY on the employee's

    A. capability   B. experience
    C. education   D. seniority

9.____

10. The one of the following situations where it is MOST appropriate to transfer an employee to a similar assignment is one in which the employee

    A. lacks motivation and interest
    B. experiences a personality conflict with his supervisor

10.____

C. is negligent in the performance of his duties
D. lacks capacity or ability to perform assigned tasks

11. The one of the following which is LEAST likely to be affected by improvements in the morale of personnel is employee   11.____

    A. skill   B. absenteeism
    C. turnover   D. job satisfaction

12. The one of the following situations in which it is LEAST appropriate for a supervisor to delegate authority to subordinates is where the supervisor   12.____

    A. lacks confidence in his own abilities to perform certain work
    B. is overburdened and cannot handle all his responsibilities
    C. refers all disciplinary problems to his subordinate
    D. has to deal with an emergency or crisis

13. Assume that it has come to your attention that two of your subordinates have shouted at each other and have almost engaged in a fist fight. Luckily, they were separated by some of the other employees.
Of the following, your BEST immediate course of action would *generally* be to   13.____

    A. reprimand the senior of the two subordinates since he should have known better
    B. hear the story from both employees and any witnesses and then take needed disciplinary action
    C. ignore the matter since nobody was physically hurt
    D. immediately suspend and fine both employees pending a departmental hearing

14. You have been delegating some of your authority to one of your subordinates because of his leadership potential. Which of the following actions is LEAST conducive to the growth and development of this individual for a supervisory position?   14.____

    A. Use praise only when it will be effective
    B. Give very detailed instructions and supervise the employee closely to be sure that the instructions are followed precisely
    C. Let the subordinate proceed with his planned course of action even if mistakes, within a permissible range, are made
    D. Intervene on behalf of the subordinate whenever an assignment becomes difficult for him

15. A rumor has been spreading in your department concerning the possibility of layoffs due to decreased revenues.
As a supervisor, you should GENERALLY   15.____

    A. deny the rumor, whether it is true or false, in order to keep morale from declining
    B. inform the men to the best of your knowledge about this situation and keep them advised of any new information
    C. tell the men to forget about the rumor and concentrate on increasing their productivity
    D. ignore the rumor since it is not authorized information

16. Within an organization, every supervisor should know to whom he reports and who   16._____
reports to him.
The one of the following which is achieved by use of such structured relationships is

    A.   unity of command   B.   confidentiality
    C.   esprit de corps   D.   promotion opportunities

17. Almost every afternoon, one of your employees comes back from his break ten minutes   17._____
late without giving you any explanation.
Which of the following actions should you take FIRST in this situation?

    A.   Assign the employee to a different type of work and observe whether his behavior
changes
    B.   Give the employee extra work to do so that he will have to return on time
    C.   Ask the employee for an explanation for his lateness
    D.   Tell the employee he is jeopardizing the break for everyone

18. When giving instructions to your employees in a group, which one of the following should   18._____
you make certain to do?

    A.   Speak in a casual, offhand manner
    B.   Assume that your employees fully understand the instructions
    C.   Write out your instructions beforehand and read them to the employees
    D.   Tell exactly who is to do what

19. A fist fight develops between two men under your supervision.   19._____
The MOST advisable course of action for you to take FIRST is to

    A.   call the police
    B.   have the other workers pull them apart
    C.   order them to stop
    D.   step between the two men

20. You have assigned some difficult and unusual work to one of your most experienced and   20._____
competent subordinates.
If you notice that he is doing the work incorrectly, you should

    A.   assign the work to another employee
    B.   reprimand him in private
    C.   show him immediately how the work should be done
    D.   wait until the job is completed and then correct his errors

———————

KEY (CORRECT ANSWERS)

1.	D		11.	A
2.	D		12.	C
3.	D		13.	B
4.	B		14.	B
5.	A		15.	B
6.	C		16.	A
7.	D		17.	C
8.	B		18.	D
9.	A		19.	C
10.	B		20.	C

EXAMINATION SECTION
TEST 1

DIRECTIONS: Each question or incomplete statement is foll'owed by several suggested answers or completions. Select the one that BEST answers the question or completes the statement. *PRINT THE LETTER OF THE CORRECT ANSWER IN THE SPACE AT THE RIGHT.*

1. Of the following, the one MOST important quality required of a good supervisor is   1.____

    A. ambition   B. leadership
    C. friendliness   D. popularity

2. It is often said that a supervisor can delegate authority but **never responsibility.**   2.____
This means MOST NEARLY that

    A. a supervisor must do his own work if he expects it to be done properly
    B. a supervisor can assign someone else to do his work, but in the last analysis, the supervisor himself must take the blame for any actions followed
    C. authority and responsibility are two separate things that cannot be borne by the same person
    D. it is better for a supervisor never to delegate his authority

3. One of your men who is a habitual complainer asks you to grant him a minor privilege.   3.____
Before granting or denying such a request, you should consider

    A. the merits of the case
    B. that it is good for group morale to grant a request of this nature
    C. the man's seniority
    D. that to deny such a request will lower your standing with the men

4. A supervisory practice on the part of a foreman which is MOST likely to lead to confusion   4.____
and inefficiency is for him to

    A. give orders verbally directly to the man assigned to the job
    B. issue orders only in writing
    C. follow up his orders after issuing them
    D. relay his orders to the men through co-workers

5. It would be POOR supervision on a foreman's part if he   5.____

    A. asked an experienced maintainer for his opinion on the method of doing a special job
    B. make it a policy to avoid criticizing a man in front of his co-workers
    C. consulted his assistant supervisor on unusual problems
    D. allowed a cooling-off period of several days before giving one of his men a deserved reprimand

6. Of the following behavior characteristics of a supervisor, the one that is MOST likely to   6.____
lower the morale of the men he supervises is

    A. diligence   B. favoritism
    C. punctuality   D. thoroughness

7. Of the following, the BEST method of getting an employee who is not working up to his capacity to produce more work is to

    A. have another employee criticize his production
    B. privately criticize his production but encourage him to produce more
    C. criticize his production before his associates
    D. criticize his production and threaten to fire him

7.____

8. Of the following, the BEST thing for a supervisor to do when a subordinate has done a very good job is to

    A. tell him to take it easy
    B. praise his work
    C. reduce his workload
    D. say nothing because he may become conceited

8.____

9. Your orders to your crew are MOST likely to be followed if you

    A. explain the reasons for these orders
    B. warn that all violators will be punished
    C. promise easy assignments to those who follow these orders best
    D. say that they are for the good of the department

9.____

10. In order to be a good supervisor, you should

    A. impress upon your men that you demand perfection in their work at all times
    B. avoid being blamed for your crew's mistakes
    C. impress your superior with your ability
    D. see to it that your men get what they are entitled to

10.____

11. In giving instructions to a crew, you should

    A. speak in as loud a tone as possible
    B. speak in a coaxing, persuasive manner
    C. speak quietly, clearly, and courteously
    D. always use the word *please* when giving instructions

11.____

12. Of the following factors, the one which is LEAST important in evaluating an employee and his work is his

    A. dependability   B. quantity of work done
    C. quality of work done   D. education and training

12.____

13. When a District Superintendent first assumes his command, it is LEAST important for him at the beginning to observe

    A. how his equipment is designed and its adaptability
    B. how to reorganize the district for greater efficiency
    C. the capabilities of the men in the district
    D. the methods of operation being employed

13.____

14. When making an inspection of one of the buildings under your supervision, the BEST   14._____
procedure to follow in making a record of the inspection is to

    A. return immediately to the office and write a report from memory
    B. write down all the important facts during or as soon as you complete the inspection
    C. fix in your mind all important facts so that you can repeat them from memory if necessary
    D. fix in your mind all important facts so that you can make out your report at the end of the day

15. Assume that your superior has directed you to make certain changes in your established   15._____
procedure. After using this modified procedure on several occasions, you find that the
original procedure was distinctly superior and you wish to return to it.
You should

    A. let your superior find this out for himself
    B. simply change back to the original procedure
    C. compile definite data and information to prove your case to your superior
    D. persuade one of the more experienced workers to take this matter up with your superior

16. An inspector visited a large building under construction. He inspected the soil lines at 9   16._____
M., water lines at 10 A.M., fixtures at 11 A.M., and did his office work in the afternoon. He
followed the same pattern daily for weeks.
This procedure was

    A. *good;* because it was methodical and he did not miss anything
    B. *good;* because it gave equal time to all phases of the plumbing
    C. *bad;* because not enough time was devoted to fixtures
    D. *bad;* because the tradesmen knew when the inspection would occur

17. Assume that one of the foremen in a training course, which you are conducting, pro-   17._____
poses a poor solution for a maintenance problem.
Of the following, the BEST course of action for you to take is to

    A. accept the solution tentatively and correct it during the next class meeting
    B. point out all the defects of this proposed solution and wait until somebody thinks of a better solution
    C. try to get the class to reject this proposed solution and develop a better solution
    D. let the matter pass since somebody will present a better solution as the class work proceeds

18. As a supervisor, you should be seeking ways to improve the efficiency of shop operations   18._____
by means such as changing established work procedures.
The following are offered as possible actions that you should consider in changing
established work procedures:
    I. Make changes only when your foremen agree to them
    II. Discuss changes with your supervisor before putting them into practice
    III. Standardize any operation which is performed on a continuing basis
    IV. Make changes quickly and quietly in order to avoid dissent
    V. Secure expert guidance before instituting unfamiliar procedures

Of the following suggested answers, the one that describes the actions to be taken to change established work procedures is

A. I, IV, and V *only*
B. II, III, and V *only*
C. III, IV, and V *only*
D. All of the above

19. A supervisor determined that a foreman, without informing his superior, delegated responsibility for checking time cards to a member of his gang. The supervisor then called the foreman into his office where he reprimanded the foreman.
This action of the supervisor in reprimanding the foreman was

19.____

A. *proper;* because the checking of time cards is the foreman's responsibility and should not be delegated
B. proper; because the foreman did not ask the supervisor for permission to delegate responsibility
C. improper; because the foreman may no longer take the initiative in solving future problems
D. *improper;* because the supervisor is interfering in a function which is not his responsibility

20. A capable supervisor should check all operations under his control.
Of the following, the LEAST important reason for doing this is to make sure that

20.____

A. operations are being performed as scheduled
B. he personally observes all operations at all times
C. all the operations are still needed
D. his manpower is being utilized efficiently

21. A supervisor makes it a practice to apply fair and firm discipline in all cases of rule infractions, including those of a minor nature.
This practice should PRIMARILY be considered

21.____

A. *bad;* since applying discipline for minor violations is a waste of time
B. *good;* because not applying discipline for minor infractions can lead to a more serious erosion of discipline
C. *bad;* because employees do not like to be disciplined for minor violations of the rules
D. *good;* because violating any rule can cause a dangerous situation to occur

22. A maintainer would PROPERLY consider it poor supervisory practice for a foreman to consult with him on

22.____

A. which of several repair jobs should be scheduled first
B. how to cope with personal problems at home
C. whether the neatness of his headquarters can be improved
D. how to express a suggestion which the maintainer plans to submit formally

23. Assume that you have determined that the work of one of your foremen and the men he supervises is consistently behind schedule. When you discuss this situation with the foreman, he tells you that his men are poor workers and then complains that he must spend all of his time checking on their work.

    23.____

The following actions are offered for your consideration as possible ways of solving the problem of poor performance of the foreman and his men:

    I. Review the work standards with the foreman and determine whether they are realistic
    II. Tell the foreman that you will recommend him for the foreman's training course for retraining
    III. Ask the foreman for the names of the maintainers and then replace them as soon as possible
    IV. Tell the foreman that you expect him to meet a satisfactory level of performance
    V. Tell the foreman to insist that his men work overtime to catch up to the schedule
    VI. Tell the foreman to review the type and amount of training he has given the maintainers
    VII. Tell the foreman that he will be out of a job if he does not produce on schedule
    VIII. Avoid all criticism of the foreman and his methods

Which of the following suggested answers CORRECTLY lists the proper actions to be taken to solve the problem of poor performance of the foreman and his men?

    A. I, II, IV, and VI *only*
    B. I, III, V, and VII *only*
    C. II, III, VI, and VIII *only*
    D. IV, V, VI, and VIII *only*

24. When a conference or a group discussion is tending to turn into a *bull session* without constructive purpose, the BEST action to take is to

    24.____

    A. reprimand the leader of the *bull session*
    B. redirect the discussion to the business at hand
    C. dismiss the meeting and reschedule it for another day
    D. allow the *bull session* to continue

25. Assume that you have been assigned responsibility for a program in which a high production rate is mandatory. From past experience, you know that your foremen do not perform equally well in the various types of jobs given to them.

    25.____

Which of the following methods should you use in selecting foremen for the specific types of work involved in the program?

    A. Leave the method of selecting foremen to your supervisor
    B. Assign each foreman to the work he does best
    C. Allow each foreman to choose his own job
    D. Assign each foreman to a job which will permit him to improve his own abilities

---

KEY (CORRECT ANSWERS)

1.	B		11.	C
2.	B		12.	D
3.	A		13.	B
4.	D		14.	B
5.	D		15.	C
6.	B		16.	D
7.	B		17.	C
8.	B		18.	B
9.	A		19.	A
10.	D		20.	B

21.	B
22.	A
23.	A
24.	B
25.	B

———

TEST 2

DIRECTIONS: Each question or incomplete statement is followed by several suggested answers or completions. Select the one that BEST answers the question or completes the statement. *PRINT THE LETTER OF THE CORRECT ANSWER IN THE SPACE AT THE RIGHT.*

1. A foreman who is familiar with modern management principles should know that the one of the following requirements of an administrator which is LEAST important is his ability to

    A. coordinate work
    B. plan, organize, and direct the work under his control
    C. cooperate with others
    D. perform the duties of the employees under his jurisdiction

    1.____

2. When subordinates request his advice in solving problems encountered in their work, a certain chief occasionally answers the request by first asking the subordinate what he thinks should be done.
This action by the chief is, on the whole,

    A. *desirable* because it stimulates subordinates to give more thought to the solution of problems encountered
    B. *undesirable* because it discourages subordinates from asking questions
    C. *desirable* because it discourages subordinates from asking questions
    D. *undesirable* because it undermines the confidence of subordinates in the ability of their supervisor

    2.____

3. Of the following factors that may be considered by a unit head in dealing with the tardy subordinate, the one which should be given LEAST consideration is the

    A. frequency with which the employee is tardy
    B. effect of the employee's tardiness upon the work of other employees
    C. willingness of the employee to work overtime when necessary
    D. cause of the employee's tardiness

    3.____

4. The MOST important requirement of a good inspectional report is that it should be

    A. properly addressed
    B. lengthy
    C. clear and brief
    D. spelled correctly

    4.____

5. Building superintendents frequently inquire about departmental inspectional procedures. Of the following, it is BEST to

    A. advise them to write to the department for an official reply
    B. refuse as the inspectional procedure is a restricted matter
    C. briefly explain the procedure to them
    D. avoid the inquiry by changing the subject

    5.____

6. Reprimanding a crew member before other workers is a

    A. *good practice;* the reprimand serves as a warning to the other workers
    B. *bad practice;* people usually resent criticism made in public
    C. *good practice;* the other workers will realize that the supervisor is fair
    D. *bad practice;* the other workers will take sides in the dispute

    6.____

7. Of the following actions, the one which is LEAST likely to promote good work is for the group leader to 7._____

    A. praise workers for doing a good job
    B. call attention to the opportunities for promotion for better workers
    C. threaten to recommend discharge of workers who are below standard
    D. put into practice any good suggestion made by crew members

8. A supervisor notices that a member of his crew has skipped a routine step in his job. Of the following, the BEST action for the supervisor to take is to 8._____

    A. promptly question the worker about the incident
    B. immediately assign another man to complete the job
    C. bring up the incident the next time the worker asks for a favor
    D. say nothing about the incident but watch the worker carefully in the future

9. Assume you have been told to show a new worker how to operate a piece of equipment. Your FIRST step should be to 9._____

    A. ask the worker if he has any questions about the equipment
    B. permit the worker to operate the equipment himself while you carefully watch to prevent damage
    C. demonstrate the operation of the equipment for the worker
    D. have the worker read an instruction booklet on the maintenance of the equipment

10. Whenever a new man was assigned to his crew, the supervisor would introduce him to all other crew members, take him on a tour of the plant, tell him about bus schedules and places to eat.
    This practice is 10._____

    A. *good;* the new man is made to feel welcome
    B. *bad;* supervisors should not interfere in personal matters
    C. *good;* the new man knows that he can bring his personal problems to the supervisor
    D. *bad;* work time should not be spent on personal matters

11. The MOST important factor in successful leadership is the ability to 11._____

    A. obtain instant obedience to all orders
    B. establish friendly personal relations with crew members
    C. avoid disciplining crew members
    D. make crew members want to do what should be done

12. Explaining the reasons for departmental procedure to workers tends to 12._____

    A. waste time which should be used for productive purposes
    B. increase their interest in their work
    C. make them more critical of departmental procedures
    D. confuse them

13. If you want a job done well, do it yourself. For a supervisor to follow this advice would be   13.____

    A. *good;* a supervisor is responsible for the work of his crew
    B. *bad;* a supervisor should train his men, not do their work
    C. *good;* a supervisor should be skilled in all jobs assigned to his crew
    D. *bad;* a supervisor loses respect when he works with his hands

14. When a supervisor discovers a mistake in one of the jobs for which his crew is responsi-   14.____
    ble, it is MOST important for him to find out

    A. whether anybody else knows about the mistake
    B. who was to blame for the mistake
    C. how to prevent similar mistakes in the future
    D. whether similar mistakes occurred in the past

15. A supervisor who has to explain a new procedure to his crew should realize that ques-   15.____
    tions from the crew USUALLY show that they

    A. are opposed to the new procedure
    B. are completely confused by the explanation
    C. need more training in the new procedure
    D. are interested in the explanation

16. A good way for a supervisor to retain the confidence of his or her employees is to   16.____

    A. say as little as possible
    B. check work frequently
    C. make no promises unless they will be fulfilled
    D. never hesitate in giving an answer to any question

17. Good supervision is ESSENTIALLY a matter of   17.____

    A. patience in supervising workers
    B. care in selecting workers
    C. skill in human relations
    D. fairness in disciplining workers

18. It is MOST important for an employee who has been assigned a monotonous task to   18.____

    A. perform this task before doing other work
    B. ask another employee to help
    C. perform this task only after all other work has been completed
    D. take measures to prevent mistakes in performing the task

19. One of your employees has violated a minor agency regulation .   19.____
    The FIRST thing you should do is

    A. warn the employee that you will have to take disciplinary action if it should happen
       again
    B. ask the employee to explain his or her actions
    C. inform your supervisor and wait for advice
    D. write a memo describing the incident and place it in the employee's personnel file

20. One of your employees tells you that he feels you give him much more work than the   20.____
other employees, and he is having trouble meeting your deadlines.
You should

    A. ask if he has been under a lot of non-work related stress lately
    B. review his recent assignments to determine if he is correct
    C. explain that this is a busy time, but you are dividing the work equally
    D. tell him that he is the most competent employee and that is why he receives more work

21. A supervisor assigns one of his crew to complete a portion of a job. A short time later, the   21.____
supervisor notices that the portion has not been completed.
Of the following, the BEST way for the supervisor to handle this is to

    A. ask the crew member why he has not completed the assignment
    B. reprimand the crew member for not obeying orders
    C. assign another crew member to complete the assignment
    D. complete the assignment himself

22. Suppose that a member of your crew complains that you are *playing favorites* in assign-   22.____
ing work.
Of the following, the BEST method of handling the complaint is to

    A. deny it and refuse to discuss the matter with the worker
    B. take the opportunity to tell the worker what is wrong with his work
    C. ask the worker for examples to prove his point and try to clear up any misunder-
standing
    D. promise to be more careful in making assignments in the future

23. A member of your crew comes to you with a complaint. After discussing the matter with   23.____
him, it is clear that you have convinced him that his complaint was not justified.
At this point, you should

    A. permit him to drop the matter
    B. make him admit his error
    C. pretend to see some justification in his complaint
    D. warn him against making unjustified complaints

24. Suppose that a supervisor has in his crew an older man who works rather slowly. In other   24.____
respects, this man is a good worker; he is seldom absent, works carefully, never loafs,
and is cooperative.
The BEST way for the supervisor to handle this worker is to

    A. try to get him to work faster and less carefully
    B. give him the most disagreeable job
    C. request that he be given special training
    D. permit him to work at his own speed

25. Suppose that a member of your crew comes to you with a suggestion he thinks will save   25._____
    time in doing a job. You realize immediately that it won't work.
    Under these circumstances, your BEST action would be to

    A. thank the worker for the suggestion and forget about it
    B. explain to the worker why you think it won't work
    C. tell the worker to put the suggestion in writing
    D. ask the other members of your crew to criticize the suggestion

----

KEY (CORRECT ANSWERS)

1.	D		11.	D
2.	A		12.	B
3.	C		13.	B
4.	C		14.	C
5.	C		15.	D
6.	B		16.	C
7.	C		17.	C
8.	A		18.	D
9.	C		19.	B
10.	A		20.	B

21.	A
22.	C
23.	A
24.	D
25.	B

PHILOSOPHY, PRINCIPLES, PRACTICES AND TECHNICS
OF
SUPERVISION, ADMINISTRATION, MANAGEMENT AND ORGANIZATION

TABLE OF CONTENTS

TABLE OF CONTENTS (CONTINUED)

PHILOSOPHY, PRINCIPLES, PRACTICES, AND TECHNICS
OF
SUPERVISION, ADMINISTRATION, MANAGEMENT AND ORGANIZATION

I. MEANING OF SUPERVISION

The extension of the democratic philosophy has been accompanied by an extension in the scope of supervision. Modern leaders and supervisors no longer think of supervision in the narrow sense of being confined chiefly to visiting employees, supplying materials, or rating the staff. They regard supervision as being intimately related to all the concerned agencies of society, they speak of the supervisor's function in terms of "growth", rather than the "improvement," of employees.

This modern concept of supervision may be defined as follows:

Supervision is leadership and the development of leadership within groups which are cooperatively engaged in inspection, research, training, guidance and evaluation.

II. THE OLD AND THE NEW SUPERVISION

TRADITIONAL
1. Inspection
2. Focused on the employee
3. Visitation
4. Random and haphazard
5. Imposed and authoritarian
6. One person usually

MODERN
1. Study and analysis
2. Focused on aims, materials, methods, supervisors, employees, environment
3. Demonstrations, intervisitation, workshops, directed reading, bulletins, etc.
4. Definitely organized and planned (scientific)
5. Cooperative and democratic
6. Many persons involved (creative)

III THE EIGHT (8) BASIC PRINCIPLES OF THE NEW SUPERVISION

1. *PRINCIPLE OF RESPONSIBILITY*
   Authority to act and responsibility for acting must be joined.
   a. If you give responsibility, give authority.
   b. Define employee duties clearly.
   c. Protect employees from criticism by others.
   d. Recognize the rights as well as obligations of employees.
   e. Achieve the aims of a democratic society insofar as it is possible within the area of your work.
   f. Establish a situation favorable to training and learning.
   g. Accept ultimate responsibility for everything done in your section, unit, office, division, department.
   h. Good administration and good supervision are inseparable.

2. PRINCIPLE OF AUTHORITY
The success of the supervisor is measured by the extent to which the power of authority is not used.

    a. Exercise simplicity and informality in supervision.
    b. Use the simplest machinery of supervision.
    c. If it is good for the organization as a whole, it is probably justified.
    d. Seldom be arbitrary or authoritative.
    e. Do not base your work on the power of position or of personality.
    f. Permit and encourage the free expression of opinions.

3. PRINCIPLE OF SELF-GROWTH
The success of the supervisor is measured by the extent to which, and the speed with which, he is no longer needed.

    a. Base criticism on principles, not on specifics.
    b. Point out higher activities to employees.
    c. Train for self-thinking by employees, to meet new situations.
    d. Stimulate initiative, self-reliance and individual responsibility.
    e. Concentrate on stimulating the growth of employees rather than on removing defects.

4. PRINCIPLE OF INDIVIDUAL WORTH
Respect for the individual is a paramount consideration in supervision.

    a. Be human and sympathetic in dealing with employees.
    b. Don't nag about things to be done.
    c. Recognize the individual differences among employees and seek opportunities to permit best expression of each personality.

5. PRINCIPLE OF CREATIVE LEADERSHIP
The best supervision is that which is not apparent to the employee.

    a. Stimulate, don't drive employees to creative action.
    b. Emphasize doing good things.
    c. Encourage employees to do what they do best.
    d. Do not be too greatly concerned with details of subject or method.
    e. Do not be concerned exclusively with immediate problems and activities.
    f. Reveal higher activities and make them both desired and maximally possible.
    g. Determine procedures in the light of each situation but see that these are derived from a sound basic philosophy.
    h. Aid, inspire and lead so as to liberate the creative spirit latent in all good employees.

6. PRINCIPLE OF SUCCESS AND FAILURE
There are no unsuccessful employees, only unsuccessful supervisors who have failed to give proper leadership.

    a. Adapt suggestions to the capacities, attitudes, and prejudices of employees.
    b. Be gradual, be progressive, be persistent.
    c. Help the employee find the general principle; have the employee apply his own problem to the general principle.
    d. Give adequate appreciation for good work and honest effort.
    e. Anticipate employee difficulties and help to prevent them.
    f. Encourage employees to do the desirable things they will do anyway.
    g. Judge your supervision by the results it secures.

7. PRINCIPLE OF SCIENCE
Successful supervision is scientific, objective, and experimental. It is based on facts, not on prejudices.

      a. Be cumulative in results.
      b. Never divorce your suggestions from the goals of training.
      c. Don't be impatient of results.
      d. Keep all matters on a professional, not a personal level.
      e. Do not be concerned exclusively with immediate problems and activities.
      f. Use objective means of determining achievement and rating where possible.

8. PRINCIPLE OF COOPERATION
Supervision is a cooperative enterprise between supervisor and employee.

      a. Begin with conditions as they are.
      b. Ask opinions of all involved when formulating policies.
      c. Organization is as good as its weakest link.
      d. Let employees help to determine policies and department programs.
      e. Be approachable and accessible - physically and mentally.
      f. Develop pleasant social relationships.

IV. WHAT IS ADMINISTRATION?

Administration is concerned with providing the environment, the material facilities, and the operational procedures that will promote the maximum growth and development of supervisors and employees. (Organization is an aspect, and a concomitant, of administration.)

There is no sharp line of demarcation between supervision and administration; these functions are intimately interrelated and, often, overlapping. They are complementary activities.

1. PRACTICES COMMONLY CLASSED AS "SUPERVISORY"
      a. Conducting employees conferences
      b. Visiting sections, units, offices, divisions, departments
      c. Arranging for demonstrations
      d. Examining plans
      e. Suggesting professional reading
      f. Interpreting bulletins
      g. Recommending in-service training courses
      h. Encouraging experimentation
      i. Appraising employee morale
      j. Providing for intervisitation

2. PRACTICES COMMONLY CLASSIFIED AS "ADMINISTRATIVE"
      a. Management of the office
      b. Arrangement of schedules for extra duties
      c. Assignment of rooms or areas
      d. Distribution of supplies
      e. Keeping records and reports
      f. Care of audio-visual materials
      g. Keeping inventory records
      h. Checking record cards and books
      i. Programming special activities
      j. Checking on the attendance and punctuality of employees

3. *PRACTICES COMMONLY CLASSIFIED AS BOTH "SUPERVISORY" AND "ADMINISTRATIVE"*
    a. Program construction
    b. Testing or evaluating outcomes
    c. Personnel accounting
    d. Ordering instructional materials

V. RESPONSIBILITIES OF THE SUPERVISOR

A person employed in a supervisory capacity must constantly be able to improve his own efficiency and ability. He represents the employer to the employees and only continuous self-examination can make him a capable supervisor.

Leadership and training are the supervisor's responsibility. An efficient working unit is one in which the employees work with the supervisor. It is his job to bring out the best in his employees. He must always be relaxed, courteous and calm in his association with his employees. Their feelings are important, and a harsh attitude does not develop the most efficient employees.

VI. COMPETENCIES OF THE SUPERVISOR

1. Complete knowledge of the duties and responsibilities of his position.
2. To be able to organize a job, plan ahead and carry through.
3. To have self-confidence and initiative.
4. To be able to handle the unexpected situation and make quick decisions.
5. To be able to properly train subordinates in the positions they are best suited for.
6. To be able to keep good human relations among his subordinates.
7. To be able to keep good human relations between his subordinates and himself and to earn their respect and trust.

VII. THE PROFESSIONAL SUPERVISOR-EMPLOYEE RELATIONSHIP

There are two kinds of efficiency: one kind is only apparent and is produced in organizations through the exercise of mere discipline; this is but a simulation of the second, or true, efficiency which springs from spontaneous cooperation. If you are a manager, no matter how great or small your responsibility, it is your job, in the final analysis, to create and develop this involuntary cooperation among the people whom you supervise. For, no matter how powerful a combination of money, machines, and materials a company may have, this is a dead and sterile thing without a team of willing, thinking and articulate people to guide it.

The following 21 points are presented as indicative of the exemplary basic relationship that should exist between supervisor and employee:

1. Each person wants to be liked and respected by his fellow employee and wants to be treated with consideration and respect by his superior.
2. The most competent employee will make an error. However, in a unit where good relations exist between the supervisor and his employees, tenseness and fear do not exist. Thus, errors are not hidden or covered up and the efficiency of a unit is not impaired.
3. Subordinates resent rules, regulations, or orders that are unreasonable or unexplained.
4. Subordinates are quick to resent unfairness, harshness, injustices and favoritism.
5. An employee will accept responsibility if he knows that he will be complimented for a job well done, and not too harshly chastised for failure; that his supervisor will check the cause of the failure, and, if it was the supervisor's fault, he will assume the blame therefore. If it was the employee's fault, his supervisor will explain the correct method or means of handling the responsibility.

- 5 -

6. An employee wants to receive credit for a suggestion he has made, that is used. If a suggestion cannot be used, the employee is entitled to an explanation. The supervisor should not say "no" and close the subject.
7. Fear and worry slow up a worker's ability. Poor working environment can impair his physical and mental health. A good supervisor avoids forceful methods, threats and arguments to get a job done.
8. A forceful supervisor is able to train his employees individually and as a team, and is able to motivate them in the proper channels.
9. A mature supervisor is able to properly evaluate his subordinates and to keep them happy and satisfied.
10. A sensitive supervisor will never patronize his subordinates.
11. A worthy supervisor will respect his employees' confidences.
12. Definite and clear-cut responsibilities should be assigned to each executive.
13. Responsibility should always be coupled with corresponding authority.
14. No change should be made in the scope or responsibilities of a position without a definite understanding to that effect on the part of all persons concerned.
15. No executive or employee, occupying a single position in the organization, should be subject to definite orders from more than one source.
16. Orders should never be given to subordinates over the head of a responsible executive. Rather than do this, the officer in question should be supplanted.
17. Criticisms of subordinates should, whoever possible, be made privately, and in no case should a subordinate be criticized in the presence of executives or employees of equal or lower rank.
18. No dispute or difference between executives or employees as to authority or responsibilities should be considered too trivial for prompt and careful adjudication.
19. Promotions, wage changes, and disciplinary action should always be approved by the executive immediately superior to the one directly responsible.
20. No executive or employee should ever be required, or expected, to be at the same time an assistant to, and critic of, another.
21. Any executive whose work is subject to regular inspection should, whever practicable, be given the assistance and facilities necessary to enable him to maintain an independent check of the quality of his work.

VIII. MINI-TEXT IN SUPERVISION, ADMINISTRATION, MANAGEMENT, AND ORGANIZATION

A. BRIEF HIGHLIGHTS

Listed concisely and sequentially are major headings and important data in the field for quick recall and review.

1. *LEVELS OF MANAGEMENT*
    Any organization of some size has several levels of management. In terms of a ladder the levels are:

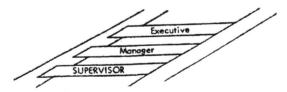

The first level is very important because it is the beginning point of management leadership.

2. WHAT THE SUPERVISOR MUST LEARN
A supervisor must learn to:
- (1) Deal with people and their differences
- (2) Get the job done through people
- (3) Recognize the problems when they exist
- (4) Overcome obstacles to good performance
- (5) Evaluate the performance of people
- (6) Check his own performance in terms of accomplishment

3. A DEFINITION OF SUPERVISOR
The term supervisor means any individual having authority, in the interests of the employer, to hire, transfer, suspend, lay-off, recall, promote, discharge, assign, reward, or discipline other employees or responsibility to direct them, or to adjust their grievances, or effectively to recommend such action, if, in connection with the foregoing, exercise of such authority is not of a merely routine or clerical nature but requires the use of independent judgment.

4. ELEMENTS OF THE TEAM CONCEPT
What is involved in teamwork? The component parts are:
- (1) Members
- (2) A leader
- (3) Goals
- (4) Plans
- (5) Cooperation
- (6) Spirit

5. PRINCIPLES OF ORGANIZATION
- (1) A team member must know what his job is.
- (2) Be sure that the nature and scope of a job are understood.
- (3) Authority and responsibility should be carefully spelled out.
- (4) A supervisor should be permitted to make the maximum number of decisions affecting his employees.
- (5) Employees should report to only one supervisor.
- (6) A supervisor should direct only as many employees as he can handle effectively.
- (7) An organization plan should be flexible.
- (8) Inspection and performance of work should be separate.
- (9) Organizational problems should receive immediate attention.
- (10) Assign work in line with ability and experience.

6. THE FOUR IMPORTANT PARTS OF EVERY JOB
- (1) Inherent in every job is the *accountability* for results.
- (2) A second set of factors in every job is *responsibilities*.
- (3) Along with duties and responsibilities one must have the *authority* to act within certain limits without obtaining permission to proceed.
- (4) No job exists in a vacuum. The supervisor is surrounded by key *relationships*.

7. PRINCIPLES OF DELEGATION
Where work is delegated for the first time, the supervisor should think in terms of these questions:
- (1) Who is best qualified to do this?
- (2) Can an employee improve his abilities by doing this?
- (3) How long should an employee spend on this?
- (4) Are there any special problems for which he will need guidance?
- (5) How broad a delegation can I make?

8. PRINCIPLES OF EFFECTIVE COMMUNICATIONS
(1) Determine the media
(2) To whom directed?
(3) Identification and source authority
(4) Is communication understood?

9. PRINCIPLES OF WORK IMPROVEMENT
(1) Most people usually do only the work which is assigned to them
(2) Workers are likely to fit assigned work into the time available to perform it
(3) A good workload usually stimulates output
(4) People usually do their best work when they know that results will be reviewed or inspected
(5) Employees usually feel that someone else is responsible for conditions of work, workplace layout, job methods, type of tools/equipment, and other such factors
(6) Employees are usually defensive about their job security
(7) Employees have natural resistance to change
(8) Employees can support or destroy a supervisor
(9) A supervisor usually earns the respect of his people through his personal example of diligence and efficiency

10. AREAS OF JOB IMPROVEMENT
The areas of job improvement are quite numerous, but the most common ones which a supervisor can identify and utilize are:
(1) Departmental layout
(2) Flow of work
(3) Workplace layout
(4) Utilization of manpower
(5) Work methods
(6) Materials handling
(7) Utilization
(8) Motion economy

11. SEVEN KEY POINTS IN MAKING IMPROVEMENTS
(1) Select the job to be improved
(2) Study how it is being done now
(3) Question the present method
(4) Determine actions to be taken
(5) Chart proposed method
(6) Get approval and apply
(7) Solicit worker participation

12. CORRECTIVE TECHNIQUES OF JOB IMPROVEMENT

Specific Problems	General Improvement	Corrective Techniques
(1) Size of workload	(1) Departmental layout	(1) Study with scale model
(2) Inability to meet schedules	(2) Flow of work	(2) Flow chart study
(3) Strain and fatigue	(3) Work plan layout	(3) Motion analysis
(4) Improper use of men and skills	(4) Utilization of manpower	(4) Comparison of units produced to standard allowance
(5) Waste, poor quality, unsafe conditions	(5) Work methods	(5) Methods analysis
(6) Bottleneck conditions that hinder output	(6) Materials handling	(6) Flow chart & equipment study
(7) Poor utilization of equipment and machine	(7) Utilization of equipment	(7) Down time vs. running time
(8) Efficiency and productivity of labor	(8) Motion economy	(8) Motion analysis

13. A *PLANNING CHECKLIST*

(1) Objectives	(6) Resources	(11) Safety
(2) Controls	(7) Manpower	(12) Money
(3) Delegations	(8) Equipment	(13) Work
(4) Communications	(9) Supplies and materials	(14) Timing of improvements
(5) Resources	(10) Utilization of time	

14. *FIVE CHARACTERISTICS OF GOOD DIRECTIONS*

In order to get results, directions must be:

(1) Possible of accomplishment	(3) Related to mission	(5) Unmistakably clear
(2) Agreeable with worker interests	(4) Planned and complete	

15. *TYPES OF DIRECTIONS*

(1) Demands or direct orders	(3) Suggestion or implication
(2) Requests	(4) Volunteering

16. *CONTROLS*

A typical listing of the overall areas in which the supervisor should establish controls might be:

(1) Manpower	(3) Quality of work	(5) Time	(7) Money
(2) Materials	(4) Quantity of work	(6) Space	(8) Methods

17. *ORIENTING THE NEW EMPLOYEE*

(1) Prepare for him	(3) Orientation for the job
(2) Welcome the new employee	(4) Follow-up

18. *CHECKLIST FOR ORIENTING NEW EMPLOYEES*

Yes   No

(1) Do your appreciate the feelings of new employees when they first report for work?

(2) Are you aware of the fact that the new employee must make a big adjustment to his job?

(3) Have you given him good reasons for liking the job and the organization?

(4) Have you prepared for his first day on the job?

(5) Did you welcome him cordially and make him feel needed?

(6) Did you establish rapport with him so that he feels free to talk and discuss matters with you?

(7) Did you explain his job to him and his relationship to you?

(8) Does he know that his work will be evaluated periodically on a basis that is fair and objective?

(9) Did you introduce him to his fellow workers in such a way that they are likely to accept him?

(10) Does he know what employee benefits he will receive?

(11) Does he understand the importance of being on the job and what to do if he must leave his duty station?

(12) Has he been impressed with the importance of accident prevention and safe practice?

(13) Does he generally know his way around the department?

(14) Is he under the guidance of a sponsor who will teach the right ways of doing things?

(15) Do you plan to follow-up so that he will continue to adjust successfully to his job?

19. *PRINCIPLES OF LEARNING*
    (1) Motivation   (2) Demonstration or explanation   (3) Practice

20. *CAUSES OF POOR PERFORMANCE*
    (1) Improper training for job
    (2) Wrong tools
    (3) Inadequate directions
    (4) Lack of supervisory follow-up
    (5) Poor communications
    (6) Lack of standards of performance
    (7) Wrong work habits
    (8) Low morale
    (9) Other

21. *FOUR MAJOR STEPS IN ON-THE-JOB INSTRUCTION*
    (1) Prepare the worker
    (2) Present the operation
    (3) Tryout performance
    (4) Follow-up

22. *EMPLOYEES WANT FIVE THINGS*
    (1) Security (2) Opportunity (3) Recognition (4) Inclusion (5) Expression

23. *SOME DON'TS IN REGARD TO PRAISE*
    (1) Don't praise a person for something he hasn't done
    (2) Don't praise a person unless you can be sincere
    (3) Don't be sparing in praise just because your superior withholds it from you
    (4) Don't let too much time elapse between good performance and recognition of it

24. *HOW TO GAIN YOUR WORKERS' CONFIDENCE*
Methods of developing confidence include such things as:
    (1) Knowing the interests, habits, hobbies of employees
    (2) Admitting your own inadequacies
    (3) Sharing and telling of confidence in others
    (4) Supporting people when they are in trouble
    (5) Delegating matters that can be well handled
    (6) Being frank and straightforward about problems and working conditions
    (7) Encouraging others to bring their problems to you
    (8) Taking action on problems which impede worker progress

25. *SOURCES OF EMPLOYEE PROBLEMS*
On-the-job causes might be such things as:
    (1) A feeling that favoritism is exercised in assignments
    (2) Assignment of overtime
    (3) An undue amount of supervision
    (4) Changing methods or systems
    (5) Stealing of ideas or trade secrets
    (6) Lack of interest in job
    (7) Threat of reduction in force
    (8) Ignorance or lack of communications
    (9) Poor equipment
    (10) Lack of knowing how supervisor feels toward employee
    (11) Shift assignments

Off-the-job problems might have to do with:
    (1) Health   (2) Finances   (3) Housing   (4) Family

26. THE SUPERVISOR'S KEY TO DISCIPLINE

There are several key points about discipline which the supervisor should keep in mind:

(1) Job discipline is one of the disciplines of life and is directed by the supervisor.
(2) It is more important to correct an employee fault than to fix blame for it.
(3) Employee performance is affected by problems both on the job and off.
(4) Sudden or abrupt changes in behavior can be indications of important employee problems.
(5) Problems should be dealt with as soon as possible after they are identified.
(6) The attitude of the supervisor may have more to do with solving problems than the techniques of problem solving.
(7) Correction of employee behavior should be resorted to only after the supervisor is sure that training or counseling will not be helpful.
(8) Be sure to document your disciplinary actions.
(9) Make sure that you are disciplining on the basis of facts rather than personal feelings.
(10) Take each disciplinary step in order, being careful not to make snap judgments, or decisions based on impatience.

27. FIVE IMPORTANT PROCESSES OF MANAGEMENT

(1) Planning   (2) Organizing   (3) Scheduling
(4) Controlling   (5) Motivating

28. WHEN THE SUPERVISOR FAILS TO PLAN

(1) Supervisor creates impression of not knowing his job
(2) May lead to excessive overtime
(3) Job runs itself -- supervisor lacks control
(4) Deadlines and appointments missed
(5) Parts of the work go undone
(6) Work interrupted by emergencies
(7) Sets a bad example
(8) Uneven workload creates peaks and valleys
(9) Too much time on minor details at expense of more important tasks

29. FOURTEEN GENERAL PRINCIPLES OF MANAGEMENT

(1) Division of work
(2) Authority and responsibility
(3) Discipline
(4) Unity of command
(5) Unity of direction
(6) Subordination of individual interest to general interest
(7) Remuneration of personnel
(8) Centralization
(9) Scalar chain
(10) Order
(11) Equity
(12) Stability of tenure of personnel
(13) Initiative
(14) Esprit de corps

30. CHANGE

Bringing about change is perhaps attempted more often, and yet less well understood, than anything else the supervisor does. How do people generally react to change? (People tend to resist change that is imposed upon them by other individuals or circumstances.

Change is characteristic of every situation. It is a part of every real endeavor where the efforts of people are concerned.

A. Why do people resist change?
  People may resist change because of:
    (1) Fear of the unknown
    (2) Implied criticism
    (3) Unpleasant experiences in the past
    (4) Fear of loss of status
    (5) Threat to the ego
    (6) Fear of loss of economic stability

B. How can we best overcome the resistance to change?
  In initiating change, take these steps:
    (1) Get ready to sell
    (2) Identify sources of help
    (3) Anticipate objections
    (4) Sell benefits
    (5) Listen in depth
    (6) Follow up

B. BRIEF TOPICAL SUMMARIES

I. WHO/WHAT IS THE SUPERVISOR?
1. The supervisor is often called the "highest level employee and the lowest level manager."
2. A supervisor is a member of both management and the work group. He acts as a bridge between the two.
3. Most problems in supervision are in the area of human relations, or people problems.
4. Employees expect: Respect, opportunity to learn and to advance, and a sense of belonging, and so forth.
5. Supervisors are responsible for directing people and organizing work. Planning is of paramount importance.
6. A position description is a set of duties and responsibilities inherent to a given position.
7. It is important to keep the position description up-to-date and to provide each employee with his own copy.

II. THE SOCIOLOGY OF WORK
1. People are alike in many ways; however, each individual is unique.
2. The supervisor is challenged in getting to know employee differences. Acquiring skills in evaluating individuals is an asset.
3. Maintaining meaningful working relationships in the organization is of great importance.
4. The supervisor has an obligation to help individuals to develop to their fullest potential.
5. Job rotation on a planned basis helps to build versatility and to maintain interest and enthusiasm in work groups.
6. Cross training (job rotation) provides backup skills.
7. The supervisor can help reduce tension by maintaining a sense of humor, providing guidance to employees, and by making reasonable and timely decisions. Employees respond favorably to working under reasonably predictable circumstances.
8. Change is characteristic of all managerial behavior. The supervisor must adjust to changes in procedures, new methods, technological changes, and to a number of new and sometimes challenging situations.
9. To overcome the natural tendency for people to resist change, the supervisor should become more skillful in initiating change.

III. PRINCIPLES AND PRACTICES OF SUPERVISION

1. Employees should be required to answer to only one superior.
2. A supervisor can effectively direct only a limited number of employees, depending upon the complexity, variety, and proximity of the jobs involved.
3. The organizational chart presents the organization in graphic form. It reflects lines of authority and responsibility as well as interrelationships of units within the organization.
4. Distribution of work can be improved through an analysis using the "Work Distribution Chart."
5. The "Work Distribution Chart" reflects the division of work within a unit in understandable form.
6. When related tasks are given to an employee, he has a better chance of increasing his skills through training.
7. The individual who is given the responsibility for tasks must also be given the appropriate authority to insure adequate results.
8. The supervisor should delegate repetitive, routine work. Preparation of recurring reports, maintaining leave and attendance records are some examples.
9. Good discipline is essential to good task performance. Discipline is reflected in the actions of employees on the job in the absence of supervision.
10. Disciplinary action may have to be taken when the positive aspects of discipline have failed. Reprimand, warning, and suspension are examples of disciplinary action.
11. If a situation calls for a reprimand, be sure it is deserved and remember it is to be done in private.

IV. DYNAMIC LEADERSHIP

1. A style is a personal method or manner of exerting influence.
2. Authoritarian leaders often see themselves as the source of power and authority.
3. The democratic leader often perceives the group as the source of authority and power.
4. Supervisors tend to do better when using the pattern of leadership that is most natural for them.
5. Social scientists suggest that the effective supervisor use the leadership style that best fits the problem or circumstances involved.
6. All four styles -- telling, selling, consulting, joining -- have their place. Using one does not preclude using the other at another time.
7. The theory X point of view assumes that the average person dislikes work, will avoid it whenever possible, and must be coerced to achieve organizational objectives.
8. The theory Y point of view assumes that the average person considers work to be as natural as play, and, when the individual is committed, he requires little supervision or direction to accomplish desired objectives.
9. The leader's basic assumptions concerning human behavior and human nature affect his actions, decisions, and other managerial practices.
10. Dissatisfaction among employees is often present, but difficult to isolate. The supervisor should seek to weaken dissatisfaction by keeping promises, being sincere and considerate, keeping employees informed, and so forth.
11. Constructive suggestions should be encouraged during the natural progress of the work.

V. PROCESSES FOR SOLVING PROBLEMS

1. People find their daily tasks more meaningful and satisfying when they can improve them.
2. The causes of problems, or the key factors, are often hidden in the background. Ability to solve problems often involves the ability to isolate them from their backgrounds. There is some substance to the cliché that some persons "can't see the forest for the trees."
3. New procedures are often developed from old ones. Problems should be broken down into manageable parts. New ideas can be adapted from old ones.

4. People think differently in problem-solving situations. Using a logical, patterned approach is often useful. One approach found to be useful includes these steps:
    (a) Define the problem   (d) Weigh and decide
    (b) Establish objectives   (e) Take action
    (c) Get the facts   (f) Evaluate action

VI. TRAINING FOR RESULTS

1. Participants respond best when they feel training is important to them.
2. The supervisor has responsibility for the training and development of those who report to him.
3. When training is delegated to others, great care must be exercised to insure the trainer has knowledge, aptitude, and interest for his work as a trainer.
4. Training (learning) of some type goes on continually. The most successful supervisor makes certain the learning contributes in a productive manner to operational goals.
5. New employees are particularly susceptible to training. Older employees facing new job situations require specific training, as well as having need for development and growth opportunities.
6. Training needs require continuous monitoring.
7. The training officer of an agency is a professional with a responsibility to assist supervisors in solving training problems.
8. Many of the self-development steps important to the supervisor's own growth are equally important to the development of peers and subordinates. Knowledge of these is important when the supervisor consults with others on development and growth opportunities.

VII. HEALTH, SAFETY, AND ACCIDENT PREVENTION

1. Management-minded supervisors take appropriate measures to assist employees in maintaining health and in assuring safe practices in the work environment.
2. Effective safety training and practices help to avoid injury and accidents.
3. Safety should be a management goal. All infractions of safety which are observed should be corrected without exception.
4. Employees' safety attitude, training and instruction, provision of safe tools and equipment, supervision, and leadership are considered highly important factors which contribute to safety and which can be influenced directly by supervisors.
5. When accidents do occur they should be investigated promptly for very important reasons, including the fact that information which is gained can be used to prevent accidents in the future.

VIII. EQUAL EMPLOYMENT OPPORTUNITY

1. The supervisor should endeavor to treat all employees fairly, without regard to religion, race, sex, or national origin.
2. Groups tend to reflect the attitude of the leader. Prejudice can be detected even in very subtle form. Supervisors must strive to create a feeling of mutual respect and confidence in every employee.
3. Complete utilization of all human resources is a national goal. Equitable consideration should be accorded women in the work force, minority-group members, the physically and mentally handicapped, and the older employee. The important question is: "Who can do the job?"
4. Training opportunities, recognition for performance, overtime assignments, promotional opportunities, and all other personnel actions are to be handled on an equitable basis.

IX. IMPROVING COMMUNICATIONS

1. Communications is achieving understanding between the sender and the receiver of a message. It also means sharing information -- the creation of understanding.
2. Communication is basic to all human activity. Words are means of conveying meanings; however, real meanings are in people.
3. There are very practical differences in the effectiveness of one-way, impersonal, and two-way communications. Words spoken face-to-face are better understood. Telephone conversations are effective, but lack the rapport of person-to-person exchanges. The whole person communicates.
4. Cooperation and communication in an organization go hand in hand. When there is a mutual respect between people, spelling out rules and procedures for communicating is unnecessary.
5. There are several barriers to effective communications. These include failure to listen with respect and understanding, lack of skill in feedback, and misinterpreting the meanings of words used by the speaker. It is also common practice to listen to what we want to hear, and tune out things we do not want to hear.
6. Communication is management's chief problem. The supervisor should accept the challenge to communicate more effectively and to improve interagency and intra-agency communications.
7. The supervisor may often plan for and conduct meetings. The planning phase is critical and may determine the success or the failure of a meeting.
8. Speaking before groups usually requires extra effort. Stage fright may never disappear completely, but it can be controlled.

X. SELF-DEVELOPMENT

1. Every employee is responsible for his own self-development.
2. Toastmaster and toastmistress clubs offer opportunities to improve skills in oral communications.
3. Planning for one's own self-development is of vital importance. Supervisors know their own strengths and limitations better than anyone else.
4. Many opportunities are open to aid the supervisor in his developmental efforts, including job assignments; training opportunities, both governmental and non-governmental -- to include universities and professional conferences and seminars.
5. Programmed instruction offers a means of studying at one's own rate.
6. Where difficulties may arise from a supervisor's being away from his work for training, he may participate in televised home study or correspondence courses to meet his self-develop- ment needs.

XI. TEACHING AND TRAINING

A. The Teaching Process

Teaching is encouraging and guiding the learning activities of students toward established goals. In most cases this process consists in five steps: preparation, presentation, summarization, evaluation, and application.

1. Preparation

Preparation is twofold in nature; that of the supervisor and the employee.

Preparation by the supervisor is absolutely essential to success. He must know what, when, where, how, and whom he will teach. Some of the factors that should be considered are:

(1) The objectives
(2) The materials needed
(3) The methods to be used
(4) Employee participation
(5) Employee interest
(6) Training aids
(7) Evaluation
(8) Summarization

Employee preparation consists in preparing the employee to receive the material. Probably the most important single factor in the preparation of the employee is arousing and maintaining his interest. He must know the objectives of the training, why he is there, how the material can be used, and its importance to him.

2. Presentation

In presentation, have a carefully designed plan and follow it.
The plan should be accurate and complete, yet flexible enough to meet situations as they arise. The method of presentation will be determined by the particular situation and objectives.

3. Summary

A summary should be made at the end of every training unit and program. In addition, there may be internal summaries depending on the nature of the material being taught. The important thing is that the trainee must always be able to understand how each part of the new material relates to the whole.

4. Application

The supervisor must arrange work so the employee will be given a chance to apply new knowledge or skills while the material is still clear in his mind and interest is high. The trainee does not really know whether he has learned the material until he has been given a chance to apply it. If the material is not applied, it loses most of its value.

5. Evaluation

The purpose of all training is to promote learning. To determine whether the training has been a success or failure, the supervisor must evaluate this learning.

In the broadest sense evaluation includes all the devices, methods, skills, and techniques used by the supervisor to keep him self and the employees informed as to their progress toward the objectives they are pursuing. The extent to which the employee has mastered the knowledge, skills, and abilities, or changed his attitudes, as determined by the program objectives, is the extent to which instruction has succeeded or failed.

Evaluation should not be confined to the end of the lesson, day, or program but should be used continuously. We shall note later the way this relates to the rest of the teaching process.

B. Teaching Methods

A teaching method is a pattern of identifiable student and instructor activity used in presenting training material.

All supervisors are faced with the problem of deciding which method should be used at a given time.

As with all methods, there are certain advantages and disadvantages to each method.

1. Lecture

The lecture is direct oral presentation of material by the supervisor. The present trend is to place less emphasis on the trainer's activity and more on that of the trainee.

2. Discussion

Teaching by discussion or conference involves using questions and other techniques to arouse interest and focus attention upon certain areas, and by doing so creating a learning situation. This can be one of the most valuable methods because it gives the employees 'an opportunity to express their ideas and pool their knowledge.

3. Demonstration

     The demonstration is used to teach how something works or how to do something. It can be used to show a principle or what the results of a series of actions will be. A well-staged demonstration is particularly effective because it shows proper methods of performance in a realistic manner.

4. Performance

     Performance is one of the most fundamental of all learning techniques or teaching methods. The trainee may be able to tell how a specific operation should be performed but he cannot be sure he knows how to perform the operation until he has done so.

5. Which Method to Use

     Moreover, there are other methods and techniques of teaching. It is difficult to use any method without other methods entering into it. In any learning situation a combination of methods is usually more effective than anyone method alone.

Finally, evaluation must be integrated into the other aspects of the teaching-learning process.

It must be used in the motivation of the trainees; it must be used to assist in developing understanding during the training; and it must be related to employee application of the results of training.

This is distinctly the role of the supervisor.

———

THE "IN-BASKET" EXAMINATION

While the exact format of in-basket exercises will vary, they frequently involve each trainee in a group first individually assuming the role of a manager who is faced with a number of letters, memoirs, and notes to which he must respond in writing within a limited time period. For example, the trainee may be told that he has just returned from vacation and that he must leave on a trip in four hours, during which time he must respond in writing to all the items on his desk.

To further complicate the exercise, you, the trainee, may be told that you have just returned from vacation and must leave on a business trip in five hours. Also, it is a holiday and your secretary is home, and no one else is around the office to help you. There are more inquiries and problems to respond to than is possible in five hours and so you will have to determine the relative priority of the work to be done.

As you can see, the IN-BASKET EXERCISE demands good decision-making skills, rather than learning new facts or acquiring new skills. The time pressure factor may result in your finding out how well you perform under stress.

When these exercises are conducted in an oral format, and after each exercise is finished (time runs out), you may be asked to justify your decisions and actions to the examiner and the other participants when it is held as a group exercise, and then they in turn will evaluate your actions and critique it. The rating, of course, is done differently in competitive examinations.

The fact that this type of exercise can be given to groups of managerial trainees is considered an advantage to management, i.e., it is easier and cheaper to administer than other training methods. This training technique also tests managerial candidates for decision-making abilities, particularly due to the time constraints involved. This is considered a vital skill for most managerial candidates for decision-making abilities, particularly due to the time constraints involved. This is considered a vital skill for most managerial positions and, although other training techniques such as role playing can also provide stress, in-basket exercises do more so and are specifically designed for this purpose.

There are limitations, too. As with in-basket questions pertaining to case study examples, they are in large part hypothetical in nature, or static, in that the managerial candidate does not have to live or "die" with the consequences of a poor decision, except where he/she is rated poorly on an examination.

Some in-basket exercises provide guidelines or suggestions for solution. The candidate may be presented with a problem which requires a series of decisions and actions but is also presented with a number of alternate means of resolving the problem, from which he must choose the best option. Next, the problem may be further developed and you may be provided with a number of new choices to resolve this new, or expanded, problem. It may even be required a third time. Then comes the evaluation and critique.

So with this technique, the trainee receives information evaluating the consequences, good or bad, of his decisions at each decision point in the exercise.

In order to properly critique the trainee's decisions, the examiner must be highly skilled in conducting the exercise and in conducting the critique. At its extremes, the critique, as with performance evaluations, can be so general as to be meaningless or be so specific that the trainee becomes so overwhelmed as to render the whole training exercise pointless.

In-basket exercises are often used in on-the-job management group training programs, together with case studies.

Made in the USA
Middletown, DE
26 January 2020